NATURISM

BY ANG COLLINS

CURRENCY PRESS
The performing arts publisher

GRIFFIN THEATRE COMPANY

CURRENT THEATRE SERIES

First published in 2025
by Currency Press Pty Ltd,
Gadigal Land, Suite 310, 46–56 Kippax Street, Surry Hills, NSW 2010, Australia
enquiries@currency.com.au
www.currency.com.au

in association with Griffin Theatre Company

Typeset by Brighton Gray for Currency Press.
Printed by Fineline Print + Copy Services, Revesby, NSW.
Cover photo by Brett Boardman. Cover design by Susu Studio.

Currency Press acknowledges the Traditional Owners of the Country on which we live and work. We pay our respects to all Aboriginal and Torres Strait Islander Elders, past and present.

A catalogue record for this
book is available from the
National Library of Australia

Contents

Acknowledgement of Country

This play was written on Gadigal, Wangal, Yuin, Gumbaynggirr and Awabakal Country. I honour and acknowledge Aboriginal and Torres Strait Islander peoples as the oldest continuous living culture on earth, with more than 60,000 years of storytelling and environmental practices. I've loved the experience of travelling through and writing on these lands—it has been a privilege.

Special Thanks

The development of this play would not have been possible without the generous support of Create NSW, Griffin Theatre Company, Belvoir Street Theatre, the Inner West Council and the University of Sydney Department of Theatre and Performance Studies.

I'd like to thank my Mum and Dad, Lizzie, Kurt, Phillip, Eve, Georgie, Katie, Madee, Julia, Whitney, Lewis, Thomas, Nathan, Peter & Dianne, Tessa, and Jake. Thanks to my agent Sharne McGee, and to my former agent Sally McLennan. Huge thanks to Declan Greene for the countless hours of dramaturgical support over the course of the five-year development of this play.

Naturism was first produced by Griffin Theatre Company at Wharf 2 Theatre, Sydney Theatre Company, Gadigal Country, Sydney, on 25 October 2025, with the following cast and creatives:

SID	Nicholas Brown
RAY	Glenn Hazeldine
ADAM	Fraser Morrison
EVANGELINE	Camila Ponte Alvarez
HELEN	Hannah Waterman

Director and Dramaturg, Declan Greene
Intimacy and Movement Director, Chloë Dallimore
Set and Costume Designer, James Browne
Lighting Designer, Verity Hampson
Sound Designer and Composer, David Bergman
Associate Director, Lily Hayman
Stage Manager, Chloe Langdon

CHARACTERS *in order of appearance*

HELEN. Fifty-five. Art academic. Bonkers in a fun way. Sid's partner.

SID. Fifty-five. Philosophy professor. Helen's partner. Self-help spiral.

RAY. Sixty. Deeply sunburnt. Guru in his own lunchtime.

EVANGELINE. Twenty-one. Lost. Amazing hair. Incredibly annoying.

ADAM. Twenty-one. Ray's nephew. Tattoos all over. Wannabe e-boy influencer. Internet speak.

TRIP CHARACTERS *in order of appearance*

STAR 1. A talking star.

STAR 2. Another talking star.

STAR 3. A third talking star.

SID-BEE. Sid, but in sexy bee form.

WHIP BIRD. A female whip bird. Inexplicably French.

NOTES

A dash (—) denotes a cut-off. A slash (/) denotes overlapping dialogue. An ellipsis denotes a trailing off.

CAPS or italics denote emphasis. Caps are more SHOUTY!

DIVERSITY PLEDGE

I implore any producers of this play to collaborate with artists from diverse backgrounds in the realisation and presentation of this work.

This playtext went to press before the end of rehearsals and may differ from the play as performed.

1.

darkness.

then: three naked bodies.

in the centre: RAY. *he is deeply sunburnt. he wears shiny speed dealer sunnies and double plugger thongs. he has a tarnished key around his neck and bears a giant tome of a book out in front of him.*

on the left: HELEN *holds a woven basket filled with produce against her hip with one hand and a pair of binoculars in the other. she looks through them, out into the distance. on her feet: crocs.*

on the right: SID *holds two mud bricks up to the heavens in his clay-covered hands, biceps flexed.*

they smile into the harsh sunlight. their voices boom.

RAY: we are naked!
HELEN/SID: we are naked!
RAY: we are earthbound!
HELEN/SID: we are earthbound!
RAY: we are free!
HELEN/SID: we are free!
RAY: and most importantly! we are naked!
HELEN/SID: being naked is very important!
RAY: for we are naturists.

darkness.

2.

bush. day. hot.

HELEN *and* EVANGELINE *stand opposite each other.*

EVANGELINE *wears a sustainable-chic outfit.*

HELEN *is naked. she stares at* EVANGELINE *through her binoculars.*

HELEN: AHHHH! that's not a whip bird!
EVANGELINE: hi!

HELEN: shoo! shoo! didn't you see the 'private no trespassers' sign / nailed to the—

EVANGELINE: / i can totally explain—

HELEN: shoo! shoo! get out of here, you textile!

EVANGELINE: it's not what it looks like—i swear i only wore clothes on the way here—

HELEN: ha! 'only wore clothes on the way here … ' but oh, actually, i do like your top!

EVANGELINE: thank you! i like your …

she searches desperately for a compliment.

your crocs.

HELEN: ah! i think you mean my *practical rubber clogs*? thank you—they're very … practical.

HELEN *looks over her shoulder.*

i'm sorry—

EVANGELINE: don't be!

HELEN: i just thought you would have explained yourself / by now—

EVANGELINE: / oh. well. i—

EVANGELINE *sticks out her hand.*

evangeline.

HELEN: jesus!

EVANGELINE: what?

HELEN: you just look like a sarah, that's all!

EVANGELINE *laughs with relief.*

but then you come out with 'evangeline'. scare the shit out of me why don't you?

EVANGELINE: … it's french.

HELEN: french! ha. of course it's french.

EVANGELINE: my mother.

HELEN: gorgeous. and she's … ?

HELEN *waits for an answer.*

EVANGELINE: … dead?

HELEN: i'm an empath.

she taps her head.

i'm an empath, i'm an artiste, i'm a professional *flâneuse*—french—i'm a bitch, i'm a lover, i'm a child, i'm a—nothing? ah—you're too young. i'm helen.

EVANGELINE: [*awkwardly repeating*] and i'm evangeline.

HELEN: you mentioned. and wait just a minute, YOU'RE AN INTRUDER! shoo! shoo!

EVANGELINE: you don't understand, helen, i've come for the commune—

HELEN: and i'm breaking commune protocol left right and centre with every word that comes out of my mouth and yet … i'm compelled to talk to you …

EVANGELINE *and* HELEN *laugh giddily together.*

EVANGELINE: oh my god, i did it! i can't believe i made it—it's not just some urban legend on nudist reddit—

HELEN: [*to herself*] she speaks in tongues …

EVANGELINE: silly evangeline! there you go getting ahead of yourself again. where do i go to check-in?

she takes her phone out of a pocket.

[*continuing*] or is it like a QR code situation—oh my god, my phone's on one percent!

HELEN: oh dear.

EVANGELINE: i know—and i don't even have a charger!

HELEN: oh dear oh dear oh dear dear me.

EVANGELINE: haha—what's wrong?

HELEN: you don't … want to stay … do you?

EVANGELINE: oh helen, of course i want to stay! i knew it as soon as i saw that gorgeous handmade sign that said 'no trespassers'. but like no pressure like no worries if not like only if you've got / room—

HELEN: / room! room! look around! we've got nothing but room!

EVANGELINE: and it's *just* like i imagined—NO—*better*! goodbye forever to my dumpster-fire life—

HELEN: then again, the chance to fucking talk! i'll call you 'e'. less confronting.

SID: [*off, far away*] helen!

EVANGELINE: ooh, who's that?

HELEN: shit, he's coming! tell me a few things! what arthouse films are on at the cinema? who's in them?

EVANGELINE: i don't really have the attention span for movies but this reel of timothée chalamet eating chicken wings did come up in my feed—

HELEN: [*jumping in*] none of those words make sense to me!

SID: [*off, closer*] HEL!

HELEN: literature, then! who won the pulitzer?

EVANGELINE: is that a dog breed?

HELEN: gossip! political scandal! please, anything!

EVANGELINE: [*thinking hard*] okay, okay … i don't know if this counts, but … the teens are making slime again.

HELEN: what?!

SID: [*off, closer still*] HELEN!

HELEN: oh, useless, useless! forget i asked. now shut up and let me do the talking.

SID *enters, bearing an overflowing basket of produce.* EVANGELINE *ogles the bounty.*

SID: there you are, honeybee. what are you doing all the way out here?

HELEN: just twitching, sid! trying to spot that damn whip bird—i can only hear the female, usually there's a pair—

SID: ahh, the *beautiful endless present* was especially beautiful and endless this sun cycle! i made an unprecedented number of mud bricks for the new barbecue shelter, then i frolicked in the food forest till my ego shrank away inside me … but—oh! i saved the best task for us to do together. let's get pickling, hel! just look at today's harvest!

EVANGELINE *approaches* SID *and the basket of produce.*

HELEN: can't wait, honeybee, / it's just …

EVANGELINE: / oh my god that's literally the biggest cucumber i've ever seen! hi, i'm evangeline.

HELEN: [*gently*] but i call her 'e'!

SID *face is plastered with a wide and uncomfortable smile.*

SID: AHHHHH!

his basket of produce goes flying. he drops to the ground and feverishly commences doing push-ups.

[*mantra under his breath*] we are naked, we are earthbound, we are free. we are naked, we are earthbound, we are free …

EVANGELINE: helen, why is he doing that?!

HELEN: i told you to let me handle it, e! now look what you've done. and he's been doing so well. siddy? if you can hear me, don't worry—i'm going to get ray!

SID *raises a hand to give* HELEN *the thumbs-up.*

EVANGELINE: yes! someone else would be great right now!
HELEN: i *do* hate to disturb him … but i'll just give him a quick call …

she calls off.

[*top of her lungs*] RAAAAAAY!

RAY *enters. he carries a hoe.*

RAY: what is it? i was hoeing.

SID *whimpers with existential angst.*

[*crossing to* SID] oh, what's happened, siddy? have you been staring at the sun again?
HELEN: ray ray! we've got a—
SID: [*squeaking*] intruder!

RAY *whips around.*

EVANGELINE: [*sticking her hand out once more*] evangeline!

RAY*'s back goes out.*

RAY: jesus christ!
HELEN: what have you done now? / your bloody bastard back again?
RAY: / my bloody bastard back again!
HELEN: assume the position!

HELEN *does an elaborate chiropractic move on* RAY *and his spine cracks in three places. he releases a deep groan of relief.*

[*winking to* EVANGELINE] learnt that in bali.
SID: *down the road*, helen!
HELEN: sorry, siddy—i learned that *down the road.*
SID: we must remove the intruder immediately!
HELEN: but ray, she's so *vibrant*!
SID: [*correcting*] more like *violent*!
HELEN: she's full of fascinating tidbits!
SID: *dangerous intruder!*
HELEN: she's french!

SID: *redacted nation state!*
HELEN: she—she wants to stay.

SID *drops to the ground.*

RAY: it's okay, sid. one breath at a time.

SID *heeds* RAY *and breathes.*

remember what we do when events are not within our control? / consult the thingy!
SID: [*finger-guns*] / consult the thingy!
RAY: go get it for me, would you?
SID: you know i love a task!

he runs off happily.

EVANGELINE: sorry, but … what's the thingy?

SID *re-enters holding the thingy—a giant tome of a book.*

SID: HAH! 'what's the thingy'!

SID *holds up the thingy.*

this! is the thingy!

pause.

EVANGELINE: okay but you still haven't really / said what it is—
RAY: [*saying what it is*] / the thingy is a living document penned by a wise and influential prophet—
HELEN: [*whispering to* EVANGELINE] it was ray.
RAY: that contains every little gem of naturist philosophy, environmental calculations and systems for harmonious living, compiled over the past twenty / years.

SID *finds two nearby mud bricks and starts doing bicep curls to self-soothe.*

SID: / don't quantify, ray. present tense, / please—
RAY: / yes, thank you, sid.
EVANGELINE: wait, you've been here for twenty years?
SID: [*faster bicep curls*] don't quantify!
RAY: thank you, sid.
HELEN: oh please oh please can we keep her, ray?

RAY *touches his fingers to his tongue and flicks through the thingy.*

RAY: now hold on, hel. the thingy decrees that even if we *were* to accept a newcomer—

SID: which we never have, by the way!

RAY: thank you, sid—that this newcomer would have to successfully complete a comprehensive set of questions to prove that they are *not* an intruder but an *insider*.

EVANGELINE: [*grounding herself*] okay, i'm ready!

RAY: are you sure?

EVANGELINE: … yes?

RAY: and so it begins … operation cooperation questionnaire!

HELEN/SID: operation cooperation questionnaire!

RAY: name!

HELEN/EVANGELINE: evangeline.

RAY: date of birth!

EVANGELINE: scorpio!

RAY: what?

EVANGELINE: i mean, third of november 2003!

RAY: [*minor back pang*] jesus christ!

SID: next question, ray!

RAY: [*quickly recovering*] are you a textile?

EVANGELINE: no!

RAY: are you a lost bushwalker?

EVANGELINE: nope!

RAY: are you an amateur documentary maker?

EVANGELINE: ew, no.

HELEN: [*interjecting*] or the sole survivor of a car crash who emerged from the fray miraculously unscathed?

EVANGELINE: no, i can't drive!

HELEN: [*to herself, 'empath' mode*] hence the accident …

RAY: are you … a naturist?

expectant pause from the naturists.

EVANGELINE: well, if by that you mean super-passionate eco-warrior *nudist* then—

RAY, SID *and* HELEN *gasp.*

wait! aren't … you all … ?

she gestures to their nude bodies.

RAY: nudists! hah! of course we're not nudists! nudists put naked first. doesn't matter where they are or what they're doing. godless heathens—they just like cooking spaghetti with their bits out. sick bastards! we are *naturists* …

he gestures to SID, HELEN *and himself.*

naturists put nature first.

SID: our naked body is just one part of this much greater whole.

RAY: part of everything you see around you. this is cool-climate temperate rainforest—

SID: safe!

HELEN: lush!

RAY: and, most importantly, secluded. here we listen, tend, try to understand it better by slowing down.

EVANGELINE: yes, exactly!

SID: we embrace permaculture.

HELEN: we rehydrate the landscape.

RAY: we take from our organic food forests only what we know we can

RAY/SID/HELEN: give back.

EVANGELINE: yes! i'm a naturist then!

RAY: no you're not! you're just saying that because we said that!

EVANGELINE: no, like, now that i think about it, i totally am, it's just, i haven't really ever considered … you know … *naturism* … as, like, a sub-culture. i mean—my algorithm was more free the nip love your mother zero-waste save the turtles sustainable haircare for ethical queens / kind of—

HELEN: / what fascinating nonsense …

RAY: [*hand up*] thank you, evangeline, that's more than enough.

he flicks through the thingy once more.

'intruder! we appreciate your enthusiasm but kindly ask that you decamp in a quiet and orderly / fashion'—

EVANGELINE: / please, i'll do anything you want—this is everything i ever dreamed of and more. and sure, i thought there might be younger people than boomers here—

HELEN: we're gen x!

EVANGELINE: [*continuing*] but you don't *know* how much i need this!

RAY: i know it might not seem like it, evangeline, but we're a vulnerable bunch. christ—we've all got our unmentionables out in the open bush—what if a snake came up and just ... anyway. what i'm saying is, the thingy helps us keep things in order, to protect ourselves and our paradise. this whole ecosystem is incredibly complex ... and delicate.

he glances back at SID, *who is bicep-curling furiously.*

EVANGELINE *starts stripping determinedly. she finds a gum leaf. caresses it.*

EVANGELINE: i *am* a naturist. see?

RAY: there's no need for that. sid—operation cooperation sub-section c, plan of action, if you please.

SID *reads from the thingy and starts shooing* EVANGELINE *with a cucumber from his basket of produce.*

SID: shoo! shoo!

EVANGELINE: please! i can't go back there! i'm a criminal!

HELEN *and* RAY *gasp.*

a climate criminal.

HELEN: oh.

SID: climahhh—crimiiiiiii—

EVANGELINE: i just couldn't handle the *drone*, okay? the air conditioner wouldn't stop *droning*—but it's not like i wanted to cause the apocalypse and i can't go back, please!

SID: [*clapping hands over his ears*] apocaaaaahhh!

RAY: whoa whoa whoa, slow down, evangeline—why can't you go back?

HELEN: [*nosy*] yes, we want to hear *all* the juicy details.

EVANGELINE *grounds herself for her confession.*

EVANGELINE: okay. so summer's hot, right? i'm working from home, and it's like, a forty-degree day. and this tiktok comes up on my feed: 'air conditioning—the invisible contributor to the climate crisis'.

SID: [*uncovering ears*] climeuuugh criiiiii—

EVANGELINE: i look up on my wall, and i see it. my air conditioner. on full blast. i unmute my phone and this torrent of information jackhammers my eardrums—like, 'do you know how bad air conditioning is for the environment?'

SID *claps his hands over his ears anew.*

[*continuing*] 'did you know air conditioners are full of nothing but toxic chemicals and heavy metals and microplastics?' so i get my air con app up on my phone and turn it off and decide i'm never ever using the AC again! but then i'm in bed that night—my apartment is literally a furnace, like, my sweat has sweat on it and i'm scrolling, begging my brain to fall asleep but nothing i do is working and it's suffocating, i'm suffocating so i think 'just for tonight'. 'just for tonight i'll pop the AC back on.' and it feels … incredible.

she sighs out.

until that tiktok starts playing over and over again in my mind and i'm like holy shit, outside it's only getting hotter which means more air conditioning which means more greenhouse gases which means more heat which means more air conditioning and i'm so selfish. like, i don't recycle my soft plastics and i buy things from zara sometimes and there are bushfires burning next to the city and up the coast and here i am with my bloody AC blasting and i've never noticed it before, but my air con—it drones this infuriating drone, like it's looking down its nose at me saying 'evangeline, you're a fucking hypocrite' so i stand up on my bed and i start droning back to see how it likes it and i want to smother it like it's smothering me and i just … grip it so hard that i … rip it clean off the wall. i uber to the tip that night. uber—green—and once i get there i throw my AC away, right onto the conveyor belt where it will inevitably get crunched up and disappear off the face of the planet! good riddance, greenhouse gases! i get back in the uber. silence. finally the droning is gone. i put my airpods in and watch the air conditioning tiktok all the way through this time … the whole three minutes, just to celebrate … and right at the end the video it says that … it's when the air conditioner is discarded … when it's broken down … that that's actually what releases the greenhouse gases and heavy metals and microplastics into the air and earth for tens of thousands of years.

she exhales breathless sobs.

i try so hard … i care so much … but i couldn't even get this right … because i'm the worst, most selfish person in the world and i'm addicted to my phone and i suck and there's like … this hurt in my—chest … it's impossible …

she starts scrolling on her phone. it relaxes her like a drug.

he crouches down to face her.

RAY: evangeline. i have to admit i only understood about a third of the words coming out of your mouth … but i think … that you have made your way to the right place.

EVANGELINE *sobs.*

we were all like you, once. we too felt *the crush.*

EVANGELINE: the … crush?

RAY: *down the road*—that place is long forsaken.

HELEN: there were some good bits to it—

RAY: [*continuing*] in a former life, i was the CEO of a climate innovation firm.

SID *tentatively uncovers his ears once more.*

[*continuing*] sid was a philosopher who thought so much about the state of our world he sent himself over the edge. which brings us to helen.

HELEN *smiles.*

RAY: well—helen's here too.

HELEN: … yes.

RAY: we went from being friends who attended the occasional nude catamaran event to committing our lives to something greater. evangeline, this may very well be the last place on earth that people like us can actually make a difference.

EVANGELINE *scrolls madly and sobs with guilt.*

listen, evangeline. you're here. it's safe with us. look up, it's beautiful!

EVANGELINE *isn't listening—still consumed by overwhelm and her phone.*

RAY *gently pries the phone out of* EVANGELINE*'s vice grip. turns out she's incredibly strong.*

let it—go—there we go! now i don't know what this smooth black device is—

EVANGELINE: ph-phh-phhhooooone—

RAY: [*soothing*] shhh shhh shhh. it's going to be alright. just listen to my voice, grasshopper. close your eyes.

she does so reluctantly.

what can you hear?

EVANGELINE: nothing.

RAY: no … breathe. can you hear your own breath?

EVANGELINE *nods slowly.*

now … what else can you hear?

EVANGELINE*'s ears open up. the rustle of gum leaves. a whip bird calls far away.*

EVANGELINE: i hear … the trees. there's a weird … is that a bird?

HELEN: a whip bird. male only—usually there's two.

RAY: good, grasshopper, good.

EVANGELINE: wow. i've never …

RAY: this is how we control *the crush*. we slow down.

SID: [*chiming*] *present tense.*

RAY: thank you, sid. we stay present. use our hands. garden. gather. preserve. build. craft—

HELEN: i keep myself busy with a robust arts practice! there's a cave just up the hill that i like to call 'helen's craft cave'. that's how i made these hats!

SID, HELEN *and* RAY *pull hats out from seemingly nowhere.*

they're so—

EVANGELINE: fugly?

HELEN: i was going to say 'organic' …

RAY: here we have everything you could possibly want and more. entire ecosystems, unfathomable universes that vibrate in every square centimetre of this place. what else can you hear?

a bee starts buzzing.

EVANGELINE: a bee? ohmigod get it away!

EVANGELINE*'s ears pick up a visceral squelching sound.*

and what's that?

RAY: tens of thousands of worms breaking down human waste in the compost!

the worms grow louder and louder.

EVANGELINE: euugh! that's … disgusting!

RAY: no, it's *beautiful*!

EVANGELINE *is in her own personal nightmare. the sounds and smells around her become like a horror movie.* RAY *outstretches his arms in ecstasy.*

[*booming, slow*] all of this could be yours … just you … and us … minus *the crush*!

EVANGELINE *lashes out and snatches her phone back from* RAY*'s outstretched hand.*

EVANGELINE: just one more ASMR haircut natural make-up tutorial tiktok explainer—

she scrolls harder and harder. her eyes grow big and glassy.

RAY: don't, evangeline! that thing's poisoning you—

EVANGELINE: wardrobe clear-out sustainability challenges funny lipsyncs koala videos algorithm ethical content one more phu-phuhhh phoooooone!

she does a final extreme scroll and her phone dies.

NOOOOOOO!! MY PHONE!!!

EVANGELINE *looks helplessly at her dead phone.* RAY *gently approaches* EVANGELINE *and plucks it from her hands.*

RAY *flips to the front of the thingy. he slides it in front of* EVANGELINE.

RAY: just try it, evangeline.

EVANGELINE *crumples on top of the thingy. her shoulders shake.*

it's okay, grasshopper. it's just the crush. just the crush.

3.

a week later. early evening. stinking hot.

RAY *lies on a sun lounge with his reflector open across him—snoring. he's wearing one of* HELEN*'s hats. beside him is a basket of apples.*

SID *whistles as he works, crossing the clearing and carrying stacks of mud bricks back and forth. he is also wearing a* HELEN *hat.*

HELEN *(obviously wearing a hat too) dawdles and looks up at the trees as she carries buckets of water back and forth in the opposite direction. they speak as they cross paths.*

SID: come on, hel. it's not a competition, but if it were, i'd be wiping the floor with you! have you done the weeding yet?

HELEN: well …

SID: and what happened to mending the pantry door?

HELEN: oh yeah …

SID: i'm serious, helen …

HELEN: you're always serious!

SID: i know it's a lot to do but we've got to pick up the slack for ray.

HELEN: i know, siddy, i'm just hot and soggy as a meat pie—

RAY *snores loudly.*

SID: see? he's exhausted! probably from trying in vain to teach the ways of the thingy to the intruder …

HELEN: what do you think e meant by 'the teens are making slime again?' this implies the teens were making slime before …

SID: stop the daydreaming, hel. let's keep on the job—we'll lose sunlight soon.

HELEN: maybe i could ask her a few more little questions … you know … what's on at the adelaide festival? has she read a recent edition of the *new yorker*? what's maggie beer up to these days? you know—things young women really care about.

SID *stops in his tracks.*

SID: enough, hel. we need to refocus our routine—prioritise the things we both love! doing the exact same laborious tasks over and over again.

he holds some mud bricks high above his head and sighs with triumphant calm.

HELEN *gets a sharp headache.*

[*overhead mud-brick press*] what's up, honeybee?
HELEN: i'm fine—just one of my headaches again.
SID: make sure you're drinking enough water.

HELEN *pinches her head and crouches down on the ground. over by the creek bed, at the base of a tree, she thinks she spots something. she crawls over and plucks something from the ground. inspects it up close.*

HELEN: [*whispered excitement*] siddy, look!
SID: enough distractions, hel.
HELEN: i think you'll really want to know about this one.

she beckons him over and shows him her spoils.

SID: are those … ?
HELEN: mushrooms!
SID: and you're sure they're … ?
HELEN: sid … how many blue meanies have we picked in our collective lifetime?

she flicks one to show him that it bruises.

see?
SID: i did used to love …
HELEN: remember back in thailand—
SID: *redacted nation state—*
HELEN: we went to that café—
SID: *the forgotten years*, hel—*present tense—*
HELEN: and it brewed its own mushroom tea! we could totally relive that here!
SID: *illicit substances, uncontrolled states—*
HELEN: oh come on, sid. let's spice things up again. go on a lovely trip together—
SID: keeping my strict routine and working hard for the collective is all the high i need, thank you very much!

RAY *snores loudly again.*

HELEN: don't you miss anything about our old life, sid?
SID: helen …
HELEN: remember that pizza shop on our street? gallery openings … or my guerrilla performance art … ooh! remember that endurance work i did in the state library where i activated my gag reflex every time the word 'money' boomed over my little PA system—
SID: it's a construct, helen. 'money' / is—

HELEN *dry-retches.*

HELEN: i made it into *the age* with that one! not in the arts section, but still …
SID: *redacted newspaper the forgotten years—*
HELEN: or cuddled up in our cluttered living room … yes … we'd make sweet sweet love and maybe there'd be a particularly heated episode of *Q+A* playing in the background—
SID: *redacted arts and cultureee*OWWWW!

SID *steps on a bee.*

HELEN *drops her buckets.*

HELEN: what happened?
SID: bee sting. youch …

HELEN *takes a look at the sting on his foot.*

HELEN: oh dear. watch out siddy, there's quite a few dead bees on the ground. un, deux …
SID: don't tell me that, helen! and *don't quantify*!

she counts silently anyway.

HELEN: *onze*. eleven. well that's no good.
SID: d-dead … b-bees …

she grabs an apple.

HELEN: here. bite into this for a second.

SID *does so. at the same time,* HELEN *picks the bee sting out.*

gotcha.

she flicks the bee sting away.

SID: we're a good team, aren't we hel?
HELEN: always have been.

SID: *present tense*, honeybee.

pause.

look out at our kingdom.

they do so. RAY *snores loudly.*

who needs pizza or performance art or *mushrooms* when you've got this! it's just you, me and the trees, hel. forever.

HELEN: forever?

SID: *forever*. so leave those shrooms exactly where they're meant to be.

SID *re-busies himself with the day's labour.*

a lone whip bird calls. HELEN *squints up at it. she pulls a teapot out from seemingly nowhere and discretely deposits all the mushrooms she can find within it.*

RAY *snorts awake.*

RAY: how long was i out?

HELEN: all day.

RAY: hope i didn't get too much sun.

HELEN: ray ray—i was thinking i'd pop up to my craft cave and motivate e with my sparkling personality!

RAY: oh god no!

he exits with his sun lounge.

[*off*] i mean, let's just leave her be till she's ready, hel—

HELEN: [*calling after him*] but i'm bored out of my brain with you zonked out and sid digging all day in that giant mud puddle.

RAY *re-enters, a little agitated.*

RAY: digging? all day?

HELEN: yeah, over there, doing the same laborious tasks over and over—

SID *re-enters, having heard* RAY.

SID: are my ears burning or did someone say 'tasks'?

RAY: [*looking off*] wow, siddy! you've really gone gangbusters excavating that clay, haven't you?

SID: all in the name of the thingy! i've been digging and digging and—

RAY: well, you need to stop.

SID: but our new barbecue shelter—

RAY: that mud puddle's become far too deep far too quickly. remember the thingy—we only take from this beautiful earth what we know we can—

RAY/SID: *give back.*

SID: you're so right …

RAY: besides there's a million other tasks for you to do, siddy—just give the mud a rest, yeah?

RAY: besides there's a million other tasks for you to do, siddy—just give the mud a rest, yeah?

HELEN: but ray ray, you were the one who wanted the barbecue shelter—

EVANGELINE: [*off*] siiiid? helen? ray ray?

SID: was that… the intruder?

HELEN: but she was catatonic!

> EVANGELINE *bustles into the clearing with a tree stump.*

> HELEN*,* SID *and* RAY *hold their breath.*

> EVANGELINE *dresses the clearing with twee natural furnishings: dried apple and orange slices, gum leaf garlands, cut native flowers. she seems very focused.*

RAY: oh! grasshopper! you're up and about!

> EVANGELINE *whips around. she's got a huge smile on her face.*

EVANGELINE: i *thank the thingy* for letting me appreciate that we face the *happy sun time* as a *collective* and in the *present tense*. *the crush* has lifted and *down the road* is but a distant dream.

> HELEN *and* RAY *clap.*

SID: somewhat out of context—

HELEN: sid!

SID: but … somewhat impressive. you … really read the whole thing?

> EVANGELINE *drops the tome of the book back on* RAY*'s lap. she continues to chatter as she decorates the clearing until it is totally transformed with twee-ness. think stumps for chairs, clay candelabras, wonky vases full of cut native flowers, rolls, olive oil, woven napkins. it looks like a dinner party for magical bush animals.*

> HELEN *fills her teapot with hot water and places it on the table.*

EVANGELINE: you know, as i was sobbing my guts out in helen's craft cave i was thinking that i, like, i don't think i've ever even read a full book.

SID *yelps and tries to disguise it with a subtle cough.*

i know that's like, a crazy concept to boomers—

SID: we're gen x!

EVANGELINE: [*continuing*] but the more i read of the thingy, the more i started hearing ray's little voice cheering me on in the back of my mind.

RAY: go, grasshopper!

EVANGELINE: yes, just like that! i looked around at all the hideous objects in helen's craft cave. looked down at my hands. and i started crafting. like, actual physical, *beautiful* things. and suddenly i got it!

HELEN: you know, e … craft is kind of … my thing—

RAY: thank the thingy!

EVANGELINE: yeah! living by the thingy is just like running a successful off-grid youtube channel but like, *in real life*.

RAY: [*no idea what she means*] yeah!

EVANGELINE: [*swept up*] straw hats and bare feet. solar-powered fairy lights adorning every tree. freshly churned butter from a cow named miracle, who's like family to us …

SID *and* HELEN *look at each in confusion: 'do you know what she's talking about?' 'no, neither.'*

[*continuing*] swimming holes with macramé rope swing, 'harvest this huge organic pumpkin with me!', converted caravans that open out to be a stage where some guy named ezra plucks at a banjo on a friday night and we're all drinking hot whisky …

RAY/SID/HELEN: [*a little confused but impressed*] oooooh.

EVANGELINE: the thingy made me realise that what i want is simple. to live in a guilt-free, happy utopia and to be surrounded by nice expensive-looking things all the time. so welcome one and all to the first in evangeline's exclusive al fresco dinner series. please—eat!

they sit and begin eating.

RAY: told you she'd come good, sid.

SID: and i'm thrilled that i've been proven wrong. well done—grasshopper.

EVANGELINE *beams.*

HELEN: as an empath, i *also* knew that evangeline would eventually make her way out of *my* craft cave. so, e—i have something for you.

SID/RAY: ooooh!

EVANGELINE: helen, you really shouldn't have.

HELEN: nonsense! close your eyes.

EVANGELINE *obliges.*

HELEN *places a wonky homemade hat in* EVANGELINE*'s outstretched palms.*

open!

EVANGELINE: ohhh! it's a hat!

HELEN: your very own! and look closely—can you see what it's made of?

EVANGELINE *looks closer.*

EVANGELINE: it's … it's …

HELEN: it's your clothes! i tore them into strips and wove them into a one-of-a-kind wearable art piece!

EVANGELINE: hahahahaha! they were so expensive!

HELEN: yes, they were beautiful materials to work with.

EVANGELINE: [*crying inside*] thank you!

HELEN: [*pained herself*] because when will you ever need them ever again, right?

EVANGELINE: [*equally pained*] yep, i'm never ever going back *down the road*!

RAY: we wouldn't let you!

awkward silence. EVANGELINE *prickles with fear.*

the naturists burst into laughter.

oh, we do have our fun! it's absolutely delicious, grasshopper.

EVANGELINE *eats too. she chews. looks confused.*

EVANGELINE: it's okay?

HELEN, SID *and* RAY *nod enthusiastically.*

are you sure? it doesn't taste … metallic? to you?

RAY: oh, that's just the way everything tastes around here! it's the rich natural minerals in the soil. totally organic—this is how good food should taste!

HELEN *has another sharp headache. she touches it with pain.*

EVANGELINE: what's wrong? you don't like it?
HELEN: no, no! just this pesky headache—
RAY: helen has an abundance of vitamins coursing through her veins!
HELEN: nothing a good home-brewed cup of *tea* shouldn't fix!

she pours a cup of mushroom tea out from her teapot into a cup and gulps it down in one, refills.

SID: you know what i think? i think we need to celebrate.

SID *pulls a CD player out from seemingly nowhere and holds it high above his head.*

HELEN: are you sure, sid?
SID: [*gravely serious*] yes!
HELEN: oh, how naughty!
SID: see! we can have fun here! we can go crazy!
RAY: good on ya, siddy!

HELEN *digs out a time-worn plastic CD case that reads 'the forgotten years: vol. 28'.*

HELEN: how shall we choose tonight's feel-good hit? feathers flower rock? draw leaves out of a hat?
RAY: perhaps evangeline could decide! grasshopper?

HELEN *hands* EVANGELINE *the CD and they all wait with incredible anticipation.*

EVANGELINE: [*reading*] 'the forgotten years, volume twenty-eight' … sorry … what?
RAY: pick a number!
SID: any number!
EVANGELINE: uh … one, i guess?

they burst into applause.

RAY: a fine choice! sid! track one, if you please!

SID *presses play and russell morris's 'the real thing' begins playing. the boomers begin to dance very badly.*

thingy section four, sub-section e: dancing naked and outside is one of life's greatest pleasures and should be enjoyed frequently! we are naked!

EVANGELINE: *ohhhh*—is this why we say *the forgotten years* when we refer to the—

RAY: exactly. usually we stay in the present, but let's face it, music back then was just better in every single way—no offence, evangeline.

SID: *the forgotten years*—vague, happy, harmless!

HELEN: there's actually some great stuff on here, too—

RAY: the seekers. daddy cool. midnight oil.

SID/EVANGELINE: *redacted musical groups!*

RAY: peter garrett kicked me in the head once.

SID/EVANGELINE: *redacted notable figure. jinx!*

EVANGELINE: so is this what you all listened to in the boomer times?

RAY: we're gen x!

the group dances joyously. they shout the lyrics to the chorus. they sing joyously out of tune.

EVANGELINE *tentatively joins in, then begins to relax and lose herself. she even puts on her hat.*

we are naked!

SID/HELEN/EVANGELINE: we are naked!

RAY: we are earthbound!

SID/HELEN/EVANGELINE: we are earthbound!

RAY: we are free!

SID/HELEN/EVANGELINE: we are free!

HELEN: [*in another world*] oh everyone! look up at the stars! they're really speaking to me tonight …

everyone slows their dancing and looks up. a swirling tapestry of stars winks and twinkles down over the naturists. the STARS *begin talking to* HELEN.

STAR 1: we love you helen!

HELEN: ooh-hoo-hoo!

STAR 2: you're the real star with those dance moves. go girl!

STAR 3: uh oh, watch out helen! we can see trouble coming your way … right … now!

HELEN: wait—what do you mean?

the stars fade.

another gust of wind—the music bends and distorts.

a dim light approaches. EVANGELINE *sees it first.*

EVANGELINE: what's that?

the light splits into two lights—headlights.

a … car?

SID: helen! where's my combat cucumber?

HELEN: [*losing it, laughing*] your WHAT?!

SID: ugh—i'll get it myself!

he runs off and returns, brandishing his cucumber.

and turn off 'the real thing'!

HELEN *cuts the music. the car's engine approaches, then cuts.*

the wind blows and whistles, deep and ominous. a long silhouette is thrown across the clearing. the shadow of a FIGURE *crunches from the headlights toward the group.*

the silhouette shortens as the FIGURE *approaches. everyone holds their breath.*

a hooded FIGURE *enters the clearing. the* FIGURE *is entirely in shadow.*

the FIGURE *fumbles for something.*

the FIGURE *holds something to its mouth and draws in long and hard. the* FIGURE *exhales a puff of smoke.*

the FIGURE *is … vaping?*

RAY: [*from behind* SID] reveal yourself, you coward!

the FIGURE *turns its phone torch on and up-lights its face.*

SID/RAY/HELEN/EVANGELINE: AHHHH!

the FIGURE *turns its phone torch light onto the group of naturists.*

AHHHH!

RAY: careful! they spook easy!

FIGURE: WHY ARE YOU ALL NAKED, YOU FREAKS?!

HELEN *is transfixed for a moment.*

HELEN: just as the stars foretold …

she touches her finger to her temple.

SID: *another* intruder! that's it—there's some kind of conspiracy forming. a plague of apocalyptic youth zombies from *down the road*—

SID *lashes out with his cucumber.*

back, back, ye intruder!

FIGURE: jeez, for a sex cult y'all are extremely tense.

RAY: we're NOT a sex cult!

FIGURE: man, that was a punish of a drive up from melbourne. fires creeping all the way up the coast—it was like fricking *mario kart* on the highway—

SID *drops to the ground and starts pushing up.*

SID: GAH! *down the road down the road down the road*—

FIGURE: and i'm fangin' for a good feed. anyone else starving?

the FIGURE *opens a packet of chicken twisties. the naturists breathe in deeply at the foreign scent.*

EVANGELINE: family share …

HELEN: chicken twisties …

SID: resist, comrades!

FIGURE: can you tell that boomer to put some pants on—

SID/RAY/HELEN: WE'RE GEN X!

RAY: how did you find this place, intruder?

the FIGURE *laughs.*

FIGURE: find this place? i own this place, dawg!

RAY: ha! impossible. i am the owner—i mean—i am a humble member of the egalitarian naturist collective that cares for this land. but if we're speaking *technically*—

FIGURE: if we're speaking technically, you can read 'em and weep.

he produces his phone and shoves it under RAY*'s nose.* RAY *puts his speed dealers on—they're prescription?*

see? property title, innit. adam w. fisher. that's me.

RAY *snatches* ADAM*'s phone to look at the deed.*

ADAM: hey! give that back!

SID: … ray?

RAY *looks closely at the phone, then at* ADAM.

RAY: you … you …

he looks closely at ADAM.

ADAM: whoa, keep your distance, ol' sunburn scrote—
RAY: adam? my adam?

RAY *rips back the hoodie from* ADAM*'s head.* RAY *lifts his speed dealers from his eyes and back again while looking from* ADAM *to the phone.*

yes … it is you.
ADAM: wait … you're not … my uncle ray?

ADAM *snatches his phone back and presses record.* EVANGELINE *twitches an outstretched hand.*

yoooo, it's ya boi—lil_adzXD.
EVANGELINE: ph-ph-phoooone …
ADAM: sooooo i was just dropping in on one of my investment properties and turns out i've stumbled upon this naked charles manson situation—
RAY: we need to shut him up.
EVANGELINE: [*a little louder*] ph-phhh-phhhooooone.
ADAM: [*still into the phone*] trust me to have a bunch of naked crazies squatting on my property, right? stay tuned for a twelve-part series: *exposing the exposed.*
EVANGELINE: algorithm!
RAY: sid. grasshopper. the thingy! we need to deploy operation cooperation!
EVANGELINE: *content!*
ADAM: wait … don't i know you?
EVANGELINE: no. no no no no—
ADAM: i do for sure … you're like famous or something, i swear …
EVANGELINE: no no no NEE NEE NEE—
ADAM: one sec let me chatgpt it—
EVANGELINE: NEEEED! PHOOOOOONE!!

EVANGELINE *is like gollum with the ring—she rushes* ADAM *and snatches his phone from him.*

RAY: grasshopper—don't do it. you've only just rehabilitated—

EVANGELINE *clutches the phone and twitches, wild-eyed and heavy breathing.*

ADAM: this is batshit insane … epic!

RAY: easy now … everything will be okay … you're a naturist, remember? just hand me the smooth black device …

ADAM: got it! you're @greenevangeline! i totally follow you!

EVANGELINE *screams like a banshee and runs off into the bush. her hat falls to the ground.*

HELEN: wait, e! you forgot your hat!

RAY: let her go—

ADAM: HEY, GIVE ME MY FUCKING PHONE!

SID: [*frenzied exercise*] we are naked we are earthbound we are—

HELEN: everything's going to be okay, siddy. breathe, maybe have a cuppa—

RAY: no, don't breathe, sid—run. now.

HELEN: WAIT JUST A SECOND!

everyone stops what they're doing and listens to HELEN*'s sudden authority.*

what if we all just calmed down and offered this kind young stranger a glass of our apple cider? what if we were to ask about what's currently on at the NGV? what retrospective has cinema nova got on at the minute? brunch spots, book signings, derivative art school exhibitions—nope, nothing, he's got nothing.

RAY: [*to* SID] operation cooperation—there's no time to waste!

SID *runs off.*

HELEN: stop, honeybee—hold on!

HELEN *runs after* SID.

RAY *and* ADAM *are left alone.*

the sounds of the bush at night can be heard in the renewed silence.

ADAM *slaps a mosquito on his arm—pulls his hoodie sleeves back down. scratches his neck. he's clearly uncomfortable in the open bush.*

ADAM: fuck, the nights are proper hot, aye?
RAY: yes, well, it helps to be …

he gestures to himself.

ADAM: what? oh.
are those trees always here?
RAY: … yes.
ADAM: and up in the sky, there's so many—
RAY: stars.
ADAM: and uh, what about all the weird colourful stuff coming out of the ground?

long pause.

RAY: vegetables?
ADAM: ohhhh. well that's g, i'll just get rid of those—
RAY: now now now just *hold on* just a minute—let's get one thing straight. this place isn't yours, adam.
ADAM: yes it is—
RAY: no it's not—
ADAM: yes it is!
RAY: no it's not, it's our communal site, adam, a remote sanctuary—
ADAM: bullshit, i haven't seen like, one remote—and yes it is, bruh, because i made schmitty give me all the paperwork—

he produces a legal concertina folder and starts rifling through it.

RAY: 'schmitty'? mr schmidt? *you know* mr schmidt?
ADAM: yeah, mum hooked me up with him because last year i got myself into a couple sticky spots and everyone knows he's the family fixer—
RAY: he's *not* a fixer, adam, he's a fifty-thousand-dollar-an-hour legal mastermind—
ADAM: [*continuing*] so i'm DMing schmitty and i'm like 'dude are there any shares i can liquidate stat' and he's all like 'noooo' and i'm all like 'come oooooon bruh' and he's like 'call me tomorrow' and i'm all like 'eeeew i hate talking on the phone 'cos it gives me mad anxiety' so i go in to his mahogany-ass office and ask him to show me every asset i own and i find *this*—

he unfolds a map of the property.

massive slice of land in bum-fuck nowhere. put in my name. by my mysterious uncle ray in 2005 … random! but so then obviously i wanted to sell it but schmitty said it wasn't worth all that much and uncle ray wanted to keep it in the family for some reason. but you know me—

RAY: i really don't.

ADAM: i always be on that grind. CEO mindset, dawg. keep your enemies close and your property portfolio closer. which brings me to here.

RAY: tell you what … you're right. this place—it is—*technically*—yours. a common legal loophole that mr schmidt and i would occasionally utilise for totally ethical reasons. but as dear schmitty very rightly told you, this land is pretty well worthless. so off you pop in your oversized SUV right back to melbourne—

ADAM: unclench, uncle ray. i just got here! i might as well scope out my place—and it's okay, i'll let youse all squat here until i need it—

RAY: need it? no.

ADAM: yes.

RAY: no.

ADAM: yes.

RAY: why are you so annoying! what do you need it for?

ADAM: my music festival.

RAY: no … no music festival.

ADAM: yeah, dawg. the lil_adz rap-tacular. made by me. for fans of me. right here. i'm gonna make so many fat stacks of cold hard *cash*—

he turns the property map toward RAY. *it's decorated with giant marker scribbles and arrows that read 'lil_adz rap-tacular'.*

RAY: so … you're only doing this 'musical festival' to turn a profit?

ADAM: pretty much, yeah. i'm broke as hell. the lil_adz rap-tacular has to be the dopest shit ever so i can ball again—

RAY: wait! how old are you, my boy?

ADAM: twenty-one.

RAY: [*relaxing*] ahhh, i think this is all a big misunderstanding, adam. you are set for life, my boy. you don't need to worry. you don't need to do anything! and you definitely don't need to put on a music festival!

ADAM: i don't?

RAY: mr schmidt obviously didn't tell you about your secret trust fund! my parting gift for my favourite—and only—baby nephew before i made my retreat. a robust series of diversified holdings to the tune of one-point-five million dollars nurtured across innummerable offshore accounts / to be accessed when you reached the age of twenty-one—

ADAM: / oh yeah, nah, i spent that.

RAY: you … you burned through your trust in one year?

ADAM: of course not … it was like three months.

RAY *is gobsmacked.*

RAY: what?!

ADAM: money's different now, dawg! it goes in like a second—

RAY: adam—i left you a small fortune—

ADAM: you gotta spend money to / make money—

RAY: / and it would have been accruing interest / for the past twenty odd years—

ADAM: / it's a dog-eat-dog world, dawg!

RAY: and what kind of dog are you? a stupid one?

ADAM: i'm a content creator and emerging rapper, uncle ray. i invested your money … in myself. i'm a brand.

RAY: you're not a brand, you're an idiot! and you don't know shit, kid! you were born with a silver spoon in your mouth. but me—every dollar i made was through wily grit and determination. i built an empire from the ground up! you need cash? get a fucking job. you like music? get a job in a fucking pub. you need to pull yourself up by your bootstraps and—

ADAM: i would never wear a boot with a strap, that's mad fugly! i'm gonna roast you so hard, old man.

RAY: oh yeah? what are you gonna do?

ADAM: *call mum.*

RAY *gasps.*

i'm gonna tell the whole family, tell the whole *world*, where our AWOL uncle ray is.

pause.

RAY: no … wait, you you you you can't do that—

ADAM *digs feverishly in his pocket.* SID *starts creeping behind* ADAM*, holding one of* HELEN*'s hats outstretched in front of him.*

ADAM: oh yes i can—see? i *do* know shit! i know how to call schmidt. i know how to call the feds. shit—@greenevangeline's got my phone, but when i find her—

RAY: please, adam. my life—all our lives—depend on keeping this bush block absolutely pristine and untouched. i need to leave this earth in better condition than what it was before. you can understand that? can't you?

ADAM: i own this place and i can use it however i fricking want! you're gonna be kicked off my property so fast your sunburn'll come off!

SID *plunges* HELEN*'s hat over* ADAM*'s head.* ADAM *yelps.*

the world is plunged into darkness. a hot wind whips up, whistling ominously.

4.

the next day. hot and windy. HELEN *drains the last of a cup of mushroom tea. her, binoculars hang around her neck. a basket of apples sits beside her.*

HELEN: [*singing half-heartedly*] come and see the real thing come and see the real thing, come and see … apple's the real. thing. but maybe … not?

she bites into it. tries to chew through it.

nope, definitely real. yeuck, e was right … this does taste a bit … off.

a buzzing begins. HELEN *whips around in search of it.*

oh thank god, the bees have returned. i was worried there for a second.

a native blue-banded bee that looks an awful lot like SID *buzzes into view. the* SID-BEE *wears a hard hat and carries several mud bricks which it incorporates into a sexy* magic mike-*style bricklaying dance.*

wow. wow wow oh wow. what a fine specimen you are—with a huge tight ba-donk-a-donk that just won't quit!

SID-BEE: buzz buzz!

HELEN: buzz buzz!

SID-BEE: it sure hazzz been lonely lately.

HELEN: i bet—you bees are becoming rarer and rarer around here!

SID-BEE: i'm in need of my queen …

HELEN: i'm free!

SID-BEE: because my brethren have been getting sick … first they go mad, then they get all disoriented, and finally end up dead on the ground in a mass apian grave …

HELEN: well i'm—very sorry for your loss …

SID-BEE: it's hard to remain calm when there's a constant buzzing inside your head …

he yanks his sting out of his ba-donk-a-donk and holds it outstretched near his head.

HELEN: [*still trying to maintain the sexy atmosphere*] you were just blessed with a big sexy bee brain, that's all!

SID-BEE: you buzz and you buzz but no one can hear you because you've lost your queen and your brothers are all dead! makes you want to stop buzzing altogether … makes you want to join them …

SID-BEE *begins stabbing himself in the head with his sting.*

HELEN: no! honeybee!

SID-BEE *collapses behind a bush.* HELEN *grabs her head in pain.*

sid? siddy? SIIIIID!

SID: helen?

HELEN: [*jumping*] sid! you're okay! so you didn't sting yourself in the head?

SID: what?

HELEN: nothing!

SID: i'm glad i found you. i need to ask you something. something very important.

HELEN: [*prematurely relieved*] oh thank god, me too!

SID: / i need another one of your hats.

HELEN: / i want to go home, sid.

SID *is gobsmacked.*

SID: you what?

HELEN: [*slowly*] i want to go home.

SID: this is our home, helen. i thought you were happy here! i built this whole place for us, brick by brick!

HELEN: we can start slow—a day trip, perhaps!

SID: *down the road—*

HELEN: we can do everything you used to love—ride our bikes down at merri creek. see an exhibition at heide. pick up some artichokes from piedimonte's!

SID: *arts and culture the forgotten years—*

HELEN: see, when you were the bee at least you were vulnerable, but now that you're not the bee you've reverted to self-censorship—

SID *finds a spare mud brick on the ground and starts packing his ears with it.*

no, no, no! not the mud again, sid. i thought we moved past this. i've held my tongue and walked on eggshells around here for too long, but there's only so many 'fugly' hats one can make! i need art, sid, i need cultural *frisson—*

SID: [*speaking loudly because of blocked ears*] i can't hear what you're saying!

HELEN: [*enunciating*] oh for fff—well, just look then!

she removes her hat. a jar of dried mushrooms sits atop her head.

SID: i told you to leave those mushrooms alone, helen!

HELEN: drinking this tea is the only interesting thing i've done in the past two decades!

SID *grabs the jar. they tug-of-war with it.*

SID: we're meant to be a team, hel. here forever, together, always present—

HELEN: well that's rich, siddy! you spend more time with the thingy than you do with me!

SID: that is not the same thing! you're—you're cheating, helen!

HELEN: you take that back!

SID: no!

HELEN: intruder!

SID *gasps, then turns back around and:*

HELEN *eats all the mushrooms at once.*

SID: [*loudly*] helen!
HELEN: fuck it—i'm going birdwatching.

she runs off into the bush. a whip bird calls. he strides off in the other direction.

curls of smoke start to creep their way into the clearing.

5.

the world is hazy and yellow. RAY *brings* ADAM *on and ties him to a sun lounge.*

RAY: listen my boy, i really am sorry i have to do this. i just need some more time to figure out how to save our land from your rampant capitalistic tendencies. don't take it personally.
ADAM: why do you even care so much about this stupid whoop whoop piece of shit land?

RAY *grabs an apple.*

RAY: really, this type of thing is not in my nature. i just love nature!
ADAM: when i get out of here you're all gonna hippity hoppity off my damn property you sunburnt senile fricking—

RAY *shoves the apple in* ADAM*'s mouth to make him shut up and exits.* ADAM *struggles in silence.*

a nearby bush rustles.

*gollum-*EVANGELINE *emerges a little from the bush,* ADAM*'s iphone bared between her teeth.*

ADAM *protests from behind his apple-gag, trying to get* EVANGELINE*'s attention.*

EVANGELINE *sniffs toward him, intrigued by the apple.*

ADAM *shakes the apple toward her encouragingly. she approaches furtively, reaching her hand out towards the apple.*

she snatches it, and ADAM *spits the remainder onto the ground with disgust.*

peeugh! peugh!! hey! hey! @greenevangeline! untie me and i can get you some real food from my car! biltong … chippies … monster energy …

EVANGELINE *recoils.*

what do you want? cash? cash? clothes? i have wardrobes full of exclusive merch that hasn't been selling too well. or … a lift back to melbourne! you're from melbourne, right?

EVANGELINE: *down the road—*

ADAM: it's okay … i know exactly who you are, @greenevangeline. and guess what—i think you're a total snack, no cap.

EVANGELINE *recoils.*

i follow you on tiktok, insta, onlyfans too. the way you're so delusional about the environment is both hilarious and hot to me.

EVANGELINE *goes to retreat.*

wait wait wait i mean … i learnt … so much … about … climate change? from you. from your #nakedtruth series, right?

EVANGELINE *re-approaches.*

yeah, who would have thought that hearing sustainability facts from naked chicks would make men care about the environment?

EVANGELINE: you … know my work?

ADAM: dude, of course i know your work. i watch your work over and over and over—

EVANGELINE: what's your favourite video?

ADAM: umm …

EVANGELINE *retreats again.*

no no wait! okay so i don't so much remember the exact point of most of your content but trust me, you're a big part of my online diet. or … you were until you stopped releasing videos all of a sudden, so what's the friggin' deal? you have like eight-hundred-k followers across all your platforms and you're out here of all places? wait—are you making content for my sun-crazed uncle and his boomer cronies?

EVANGELINE: [*gripping the phone*] *ignore him*, evangeline … you've just found peace for the first time. what would ray say … slow down, grasshopper …

ADAM: my uncle ray? fatcat CEO uncle ray?

EVANGELINE: um. no. gentle eco-warrior ray. caring collective member ray.

ADAM: dude, you have the wrong ray. he's a multimillionaire with a dark past … that's why he's here—he like, full-on ghosted from court back in 2005 …

EVANGELINE: what?

ADAM: what was it that he did? i always tuned out whenever mum talked about it 'cos it wasn't relevant to my life … but the feds definitely wanted to send him to the can … that's prison.

EVANGELINE: you're, like, kidding me, right?

ADAM: i have been told by many people that i am not funny. but my point is, don't work for my shady uncle, come work for me! untie me and you can officially come on board for my music festival! my land, your massive platform. it would be the ultimate creator collab!

EVANGELINE *turns to leave one last time.*

at least let me pitch, okay? picture this.

EVANGELINE *isn't picturing it.*

i said … picture this …

EVANGELINE *closes her eyes.*

for the low, low price of two thousand bucks, a helicopter drops you off at an undisclosed, untouched paradise. for one exclusive weekend it's just you and australia's most elite tastemakers. bam—oxygen cocktails on arrival. bam—michelin star drug dealer tents. bam—VR conferences about urgent issues like NFTs—

EVANGELINE: [*becoming swept up in the fantasy*] or how content creators actually can address the climate crisis—

ADAM: sure, that could be down the very bottom of the line up—

EVANGELINE: yoga at dawn … zero-waste workshops … solar-powered fairy lights adorning every tree!

ADAM: whatever! and then bam—the festival's headline act. there's this crazy laser light show, everyone's waiting … and then i rise up through the floor and i'm rapping and the crowd goes absolutely apeshit—

he starts freestyling rap.

oontz, oontz, oontz, oontz, oontz—THIS THE FREESTYLE
oontz, oontz—oontz, yeah—oontz—

EVANGELINE *looks confused.*

[*finally finding the words*] everybody always think i'm crazy …
oontz … world through pradas … no guccis … world through guccis lookin' so damn hazy
oontz, oontz, so depressed but people call me …

EVANGELINE: [*helping*] lazy?

ADAM: people call me lazy
just a sick sad boi in some sick sad days yeah.

EVANGELINE*'s face is frozen in a horrified expression.*

EVANGELINE: [*dead-serious*] that was … so good.

ADAM *breathes out, amazed at his own talent.*

ADAM: yep. it's my gift.

EVANGELINE: a utopia … full of nice expensive things … converted caravans … hot whisky … my cow named miracle …

ADAM: you're a fricking *asset*, @greenevangeline. do these crusty boomers know that? let's do something that actually *means something*, for *actual* young people. all you have to do is untie me.

EVANGELINE *hurriedly begins to untie* ADAM. *she gives him his phone back—he unlocks it and it starts dinging incessantly with notifications.*

EVANGELINE: deal, but you have to promise me that the festival is one hundred percent ethical and zero-waste ohmigod i am starving … got any more chicken twisties?

ADAM: dude, i have like a whole seven-eleven in my car.

he scrolls manically. PING.

ugh, what skibidi-ass bullshit is this? 'RFS: watch and act'.

EVANGELINE: wait, RFS … i know that …

ADAM: what, is it a club night or something?

EVANGELINE: *no*, adam! RFS as in *royal fire service* … 'watch and act' as in / bushfire—

ADAM: / words!
sorry, yeah, what you said.

they look at ADAM*'s phone. look at each other.*

holy shit … we need to yeet right now!

EVANGELINE: we should tell the others!

ADAM: meh …
EVANGELINE: what is *wrong* with you?
ADAM: okay fine!

ADAM reaches in his pocket for his car keys.

wait—where the frick are my keys?

a crack of lightning flashes and RAY appears.

RAY: looking … for these?

he dangles ADAM's keys in the air.

ADAM and EVANGELINE scream.

another flash of lightning. SID appears with two of HELEN's hats upraised.

i can't let your gas guzzler spew out any more emissions on my watch, can i?

SID lurches. ADAM and EVANGELINE scream again. flash of lightning. darkness.

6.

late afternoon. the wind is blowing erratically, this way and that. the air is smoky.

HELEN birdwatches angrily as she walks deeper into the bush.

HELEN: wooooOOP! woooooP!

HELEN's head spikes with pain.

agh! of course the headache kicks in now. come on, whip birds. now would be the perfect time for you to reveal yourself to your friend helen!

a chorus of whip birds calls around her.

suddenly, she feels feather-light.

huuuh—huuuh—wooooOOP!

she whips like a whip bird. she laughs wildly.

wait a minute. i'm a whip bird.
and i have wings!

HELEN *begins to fly. a smoky golden haze fills the air the higher she climbs.*

i'm a bird! i'm a plane!

HELEN *faces back.*

suck shit, sid! i don't need you. now that i'm a bird i can fly the coop! i'm gonna migrate down to the NGV—or better yet, the louvre! back to my tenured university job, back to my critically-ambivalent performance art career—anywhere but here!

the haze grows thicker.

hard to see through all this haze though. hard to … breathe … too …

she starts coughing. her flapping slows. she loses consciousness. she starts falling.

HELEN *lands in a giant nest, perched in the branches of a tall gum tree.*

a tooting noise sounds from far away. HELEN *rouses and grabs for her pair of binoculars, whipping occasionally to attract attention.*

whip bird! female! finally!

the tooting becomes deafening as it approaches.

huge!

she gawps as a giant bird lands on the nest.

the WHIP BIRD *drops a giant worm into* HELEN*'s arms.*

WHIP BIRD: [*bad french accent*] i brought you a present.

HELEN: oh … thank you! it's just what i wanted! wow … i am really tripping balls right now.

WHIP BIRD: oui oui.

HELEN: french?

WHIP BIRD: my muzzer.

HELEN: magnifique! it's so nice to finally see you up close.

WHIP BIRD: us birds—we like looking at you. your mate also.

HELEN: sid?

WHIP BIRD: oui. out in ze bush. crying and exercising and masturbating all at ze same time.

HELEN: yes, things have gotten a bit out of hand …
WHIP BIRD: needless to say, we prefer watching you.
HELEN: you do?

HELEN *starts tearing up.*

WHIP BIRD: why do you leak?
HELEN: it's just nice to have an audience.

she dries her eyes with the worm.

where's *your* partner? why aren't you together?
WHIP BIRD: i go off by myself a lot. looking for food. ze bugs, zey disappear from zis place.
HELEN: yes, i've noticed. the dead bees.
WHIP BIRD: life in zeez trees was not always so 'ard. before ze 'ole in ze ground. before ze old red man come wiv ze diggers and ze trucks it was paradise—
HELEN: old red man? you mean ray?
WHIP BIRD: oui … 'im. 'e come wit all ze dead square beasts.
HELEN: dead … square beasts?
WHIP BIRD: ze dead square beasts, zey pile up and up and he build his nest on top. but ze 'orrible smell come and ze liquid bubble up and ze insects scream. now lots of us 'ave gone elsewhere, see if it's better.
HELEN: oh, i'm so sorry … what has ray *done*?
WHIP BIRD: we must fly now. it is too dangerous 'ere.

the WHIP BIRD *points just over the hill.* HELEN *peers out of the nest.*

HELEN: [*gobsmacked*] oh my god … that fire has really come out of nowhere.
WHIP BIRD: what are you talking about? ze trees 'ave been burning all summer. je suis fatiguée.
HELEN: i need to tell my mate. tell everyone! excusez-moi? how do i get down?
WHIP BIRD: easy. just spread your wings.
HELEN: if you're sure—un, deux, trois!

HELEN *spreads her arms and jumps from the nest.*

7.

SID *rips* HELEN*'s hats off* ADAM *and* EVANGELINE*'s heads. they are both tied to sun lounges.* SID *crouches next to the CD player and feverishly reads through the thingy, doing bicep curls with mud bricks.*

RAY *calmly peels apples.*

a hot wind brings more smoke into the clearing—the sky has turned orange.

lightning flashes. thunder follows.

RAY: ah, it looks like we're finally getting a much-needed summer storm!

EVANGELINE: ray ray! sid! please let us go!

SID: quiet, intruder!

EVANGELINE: ray, you don't understand—it's not a storm, there's a *fire* coming—

SID: [*shaky*] fiyahhhhhhh—

RAY: [*interjecting*] there's absolutely nothing to worry about, siddy.

ADAM: i'm too young and hot to die! let me go and i'll leave y'all alone forever! i promise i won't say shit—

RAY: i'm sorry, but going back *down the road* is no longer an option.

EVANGELINE: you can't hold us hostage forever!

RAY: oh we won't hold you hostage. you'll remain willingly, in humble service of the collective! sid? send operation cooperation into its advanced phases!

SID: you know i love a task.

another flash of lightning. SID *retrieves a hand-made wooden lock-box that reads 'operation cooperation'.* RAY *unlocks it and takes out a torch, a pinwheel and a ribbon on a stick—like the ones that rhythmic gymnasts and little children use.*

RAY: grasshopper … it's such a shame that it has to come to this. in just a short time here i saw you make real progress. commune with nature. discover a cause greater than yourself. i thought that's what you wanted.

EVANGELINE *pouts—this hurts.*

EVANGELINE: i did … i do …

RAY: turns out you're as skin-deep as my unfortunate nephew.

EVANGELINE/ADAM: hey! / come on, man.

RAY: track one, if you please, siddy.

> SID *presses play on the CD player and 'the real thing' starts blasting.*

grasshoppers, all that matters from now on is … we are naked. we are earthbound. we are free.

> SID *and* RAY *repeat this mantra ominously as they spin the pinwheel in front of the torch and indulge in rhythmic gymnastics respectively.*

SID: [*totally deafened, beaming*] we are naked! we are earthbound! we are free!

ADAM: it's … it's … brainwashing!

EVANGELINE: really, ray? how stupid do you think we are? that will never work—

ADAM: *we are naked we are earthbound we are free we are naked we are earthbound we are—*

EVANGELINE: [*sighing*] oh my god …

RAY: the thingy really is more powerful than i thought. go, ray ray!

> *another flash of lightning, crash of thunder—shorter intervals this time.*

HELEN: [*off*] WHHHIIPPP! SIIIIID!

SID: helen?

HELEN: [*off*] HEEELLLP!

SID: shit! HELEN!

> HELEN *enters. she is whipping, coughing and howling in pain. both of her arms are broken.*

HELEN: my wings are broken!

RAY: jesus christ!

SID: oh honeybee, i'm so sorry!

> *the closest lightning and thunder flash yet cracks nearby.*

RAY: perhaps we should commence the thingy's lockdown procedure … we can wait out this *perfectly normal* summer storm in helen's craft cave, / patch you up with some of your materials—

HELEN: [*through her coughing*] / no no no no—FIRE! right over there! we need to evacuate. now!

EVANGELINE: [*wriggling*] yes, let's all get in adam's car—

HELEN: oooh, i call shotgun!

SID: [*becoming overwhelmed*] f-f-fffiyah?

RAY: *don't worry*, sid. and don't you worry either, helen! it's like everyone has forgotten that this is cool-climate temperate rainforest! scientifically it does not burn—

HELEN: well i scientifically observed a bushfire roaring just over that hill! don't sell me bullshit, ray!

SID: helen! i haven't seen you this upset since someone called you a kmart marina abramovic!

HELEN: he's buried something, sid, the whip bird told me!

SID: the whip bird told you?

HELEN: the dead square beasts have leaked into the soil—that's why all the bees have been dying, why all our gorgeous organic produce tastes like exhaust pipe—

RAY: helen, nothing you're saying is making sense.

SID: she's tripping!

RAY: *what?*

SID: on mushrooms …

RAY: helen, you know perfectly well that the thingy bans all—

SID: *illicit substances!*

HELEN: oh shove you and the thingy, ray. please, believe me, sid—

SID *whimpers with overwhelm.*

EVANGELINE: believe her, sid! we need to escape this fire!

SID: [*self-soothing*] *we are naked we are earthbound*—

RAY: they're trying to contaminate your mind, sid!

ADAM: [*brainwashed and crying*] ooh mow ma mow mow—

SID: GAHHH!

SID *yawps and runs off.*

lightning crashes once more.

RAY: i can see that everyone's getting a little carried away, but if we all shut up and listen to me— we have absolutely nothing to worry about! here—lockdown protocol forty-seven. sid, go cover the gardens!

the wind blows smoke and twistie packets sideways.

EVANGELINE: listen to helen, ray! can't you smell the smoke? anyone can see there's a bushfire approaching!

off, SID *cries a blood-curdling yawp.*

he re-enters. SID *holds an air conditioning unit high above his head. it is totally decayed—it drips toxic fluid.*

lightning and thunder crack simultaneously, freezing the revelation like a flash picture.

SID *hurls the air conditioner to the ground.*

HELEN: the dead square beasts …

EVANGELINE: it's … it's … an air conditioner! WHAT?!

RAY: there's a very simple and eco-conscious explanation for that!

HELEN: you *did* believe me, siddy! where'd you find that?

SID: i dug it out of my *mud puddle.*

lightning and thunder crash again.

EVANGELINE: ray, you weren't a climate innovator … you were an air conditioning CEO!

SID *whimpers with confusion.* HELEN *gasps.*

RAY: you've got it all wrong, my friends! this is a one-off anomaly, a hilarious anecdote we'll all laugh about later over a glass of apple cider—

EVANGELINE: [*gravely serious*] how many air conditioners are down there?

RAY: ohh, i don't know, a couple … ?

EVANGELINE: how. many?

RAY: a couple, okay?!

HELEN: the whip bird said you buried dead square beasts as far as the eye could see!

EVANGELINE: HOW MANY AIR CONDITIONERS ARE DOWN THERE, RAY?

RAY: a couple hundred thousand … at least …

the others react with varying degrees of despair and confusion.

SID: [*finally joining the dots*] you let me believe that this place was safe, ray! that the thingy was the solution to all of *our*—eco-worries!

RAY: it *is* safe—

EVANGELINE: you personally dumped enough old, broken air conditioners to release a whole *nation's* worth of greenhouse gases—

RAY: waste management in the business world is—

HELEN: not to mention all the toxic waste and heavy metals and microplastics. our food is *poison*—

RAY: only slightly, probably!

HELEN: *why*, ray?

EVANGELINE: isn't it obvious? to save *money*—

HELEN *dry-retches a little.*

SID: you turned me against myself. turned me against helen!

HELEN: you are a *terrible person*, ray!

EVANGELINE: you are a *climate criminal*!

RAY: no! … yes, i did dump the units. but that's why i needed to rehabilitate this land. that's why i wrote the thingy! i needed to fix what i had done back in *the forgotten years* … back then, i was just a poor dumb kid with a mind for business and a bod for tanning. and air conditioning … air conditioning was the clean technology of the future! but by the twenty-first century … the science … and the government … finally caught up and i was up to my neck in these awful, stupid, evil, dead machines! unsolvable toxic knots too complex to take apart … but this place, everything we've built here, this is *the real thing*! i know it sounds crazy but i *am* a naturist, i really am. i really did try to create something beautiful from my worst mistake … but the air conditioners haunted me … *continue* to haunt me …

he looks around at his red smoky world.

oh god, what have i done?

RAY *crumples.*

it hurts—right in my chest. *the crush.*

long, devastating pause. the crackle of approaching fire sounds.

sid, helen—you know that in my soul … i am good. don't you?

RAY *sobs. the wind howls around him. thunder clap. twisties packets swirl.*

SID *approaches* RAY. *for a moment, it looks like he might give him a hug.*

SID *extends his hand.*

car keys. now. present tense.

RAY *can't look at him. he hands him the keys.*

SID *unties* ADAM.

alright, kid, let's drive.

SID *tries to give* ADAM *the keys but they drop to the ground.* ADAM *doesn't move.*

ADAM: [*brainwashed*] *we are naked, we are earthbound, we are free.*
RAY: adam, snap out of it. please go to safety.
EVANGELINE: allow me. oi, lil_adzXD! oontz. oontz. oontz.
ADAM: [*slowly finding the words*] ooh mow ma mow mow … ooh mow … oontz … . oontz oontz … oontz. oontz. OONTZ. OONTZ.
everybody always think i'm crazy
world through gucci's lookin'—what the hell, this isn't the festival? oh shit we gotta get outta here!

the fire is closing in.

SID *faces the chaos. breathes it in.*

SID: look around. all our hard work. all for nothing!
HELEN: that's not true, siddy! we did make a difference—on the surface. kind of.
SID: i have to put on clothes?
ADAM: there's heaps of epic designer merch in my car. it's all for sale by the way, you guys got cash?
SID: how can i return back *down the road*, after all this time?
HELEN: we can go on a new adventure, siddy! maybe a little coastal town with a small gentrified arts scene.
SID: we could build a mud brick house somewhere.
HELEN: and you can go to therapy!

SID *calls like a whip bird.* HELEN *toots in response.*

everyone runs to the car except RAY, *who takes* ADAM*'s place on the sun lounge and opens his reflector.*

ADAM: come on dude. stop being cringe.

RAY: this is what i deserve. let me burn on my combed-over hellscape.

ADAM: much as it sucks … you are my family. i'm not losing my surprise uncle today.

RAY: leave this place! let me be.

this just makes RAY *sob harder.*

a burning branch falls.

ADAM: fuck it. see you in hell, uncle ray!

he and EVANGELINE *run off.*

the clearing fills with smoke. a gum tree catches fire.

RAY *breathes out and tans, reflector shaking.*

RAY: you've made your bed, ray. now lie in it.

RAY *sob-coughs as his lungs fill up with smoke.*

the car's engine starts up and drives away.

then:

the engine cuts.

SID *and* ADAM *back into the clearing and pick* RAY *up. as they run back toward the car, the clearing is enveloped in crackling, fiery darkness.*

8.

some time later.

ADAM *and* EVANGELINE *stand opposite each other, fully clothed. the 'paradise' around them is now burnt. it still smokes in places. they look for a long time at the charred devastation.*

a cool breeze blows. EVANGELINE *looks up at the sky.*

ADAM: soooo i'm thinking it might take a little longer than anticipated for me to get the music festival up and running.

EVANGELINE: yeah no shit. look at this place.

ADAM: yeah but also like, the money. i'm like, dead broke, for real. i need to … maybe like …

he shudders.

get a real job for a bit.

EVANGELINE: what, like bitcoin or something?

ADAM: nah … i was thinking i could work in a pub.

EVANGELINE: a pub … huh. maybe i could work at a pub.

ADAM: and maybe … when we start making a bit of cheddar … maybe we could rehabilitate the land as part of the marketing for the music festival? '@greenevangeline goes bush'.

EVANGELINE: i dunno if there's any point. this place is pretty … well … fucked.

ADAM: nah … i feel like nature's pretty good at bouncing back. weeds like, grow in my bathroom at home.

EVANGELINE *shakes her head in disbelief.*

ADAM: hey, that was some crazy shit we went through! i've like, never actually been like, that up close to anything that real and powerful before. i've got content for dayzzzz.

EVANGELINE: [*looking out*] yeah … i'm kinda the opposite. i don't wanna think about content ever again. or at least, for the next seventy-two-hour media cycle.

pause.

i just think about the animals. and the plants. the insects. us. the hugeness of it all. it hurts.

pause.

ADAM: yeah. i get it.

EVANGELINE: really?

ADAM *shrugs.*

pause.

EVANGELINE *starts taking her clothes off.*

ADAM *looks at her.*

is this okay?

ADAM *nods.* EVANGELINE *stands naked. she closes her eyes.*

then, ADAM *starts to disrobe.*

why are you doing that?

ADAM: i just … want to see what it feels like. don't tell anyone okay?

he joins her and closes his eyes too.

eugh! i can feel the wind on my nutsack! yuck! the ground's all dirty—i swear there's like worms under my feet—

he shudders with disgust.

eeeeuurghghhhh!!

EVANGELINE: it's okay, dude. i can't believe i'm saying this but … focus on yourself for a second.

pause.

breathe.

they breathe in sync.

[*quietly*] what can you hear?

ADAM: nothing.

pause.

wait, no. i hear … the trees. sounds like the ocean.

EVANGELINE: notice anything?

ADAM: i can still smell smoke … and i know the ground i'm on is like, totally toxic … but i feel … good? question mark?

the cool breeze blows again.

like, the breeze on my skin is cool now.

EVANGELINE: after all that hot wind.

ADAM: how do you feel?

pause.

EVANGELINE: sad.

ADAM: yeah?

EVANGELINE: yeah. really, really, sad.

ADAM *nods.* EVANGELINE *sighs.*

we are naked, we are / earthbound-—

ADAM: / oi. nah. don't do that.

EVANGELINE: okay.

ADAM: let's just … let's just stand here.

they do so.

let's just stand here, and be quiet, and listen for a bit.

silence.

then: the breeze rustles through some unburnt treetops. the sound of a bee buzzing, far away.

then: a whip bird starts tooting. it toots for a while.

its partner whips in response.

THE END

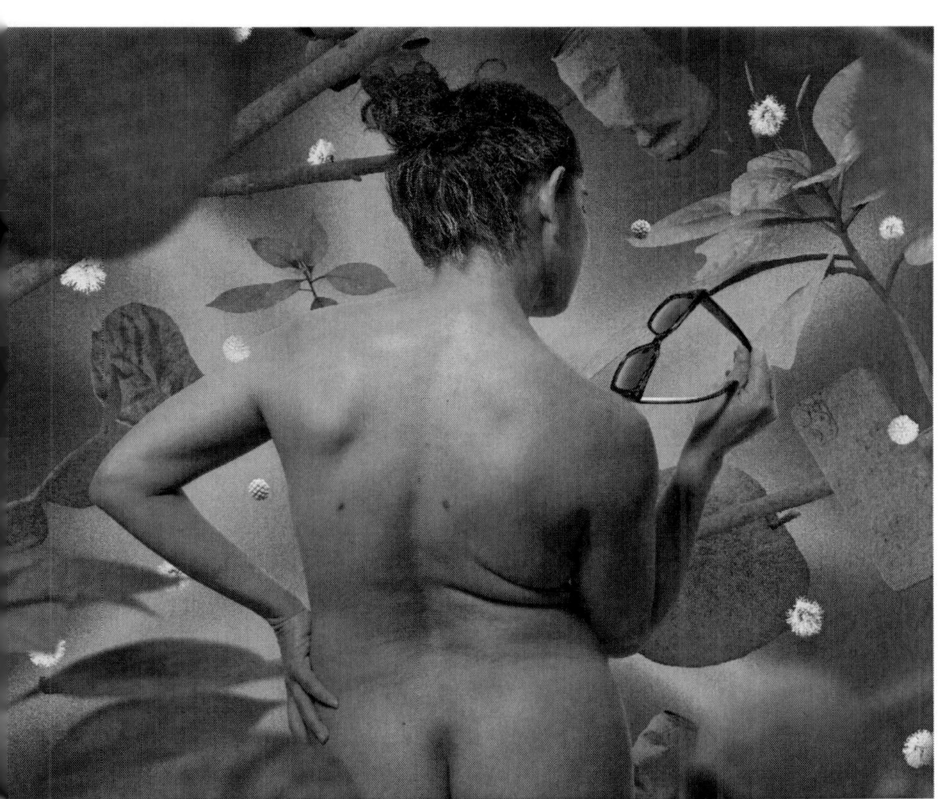

RIFFIN THEATRE COMPANY PRESENTS
ASSOCIATION WITH SYDNEY THEATRE COMPANY

NATURISM

Y ANG COLLINS

5 OCT – 15 NOV 2025
WHARF 2 THEATRE, SYDNEY THEATRE COMPANY

RIFFIN
HEATRE
OMPANY

CAST & CREATIVES

Director & Dramaturg Declan Greene
Intimacy & Movement Director Chloë Dallimore
Designer James Browne
Lighting Designer Verity Hampson
Composer & Sound Designer David Bergman
Associate Director Lily Hayman
Stage Manager Chloe Langdon

With Nicholas Brown, Glenn Hazeldine, Fraser Morrison, Camila Ponte Alvarez, Hannah Waterman

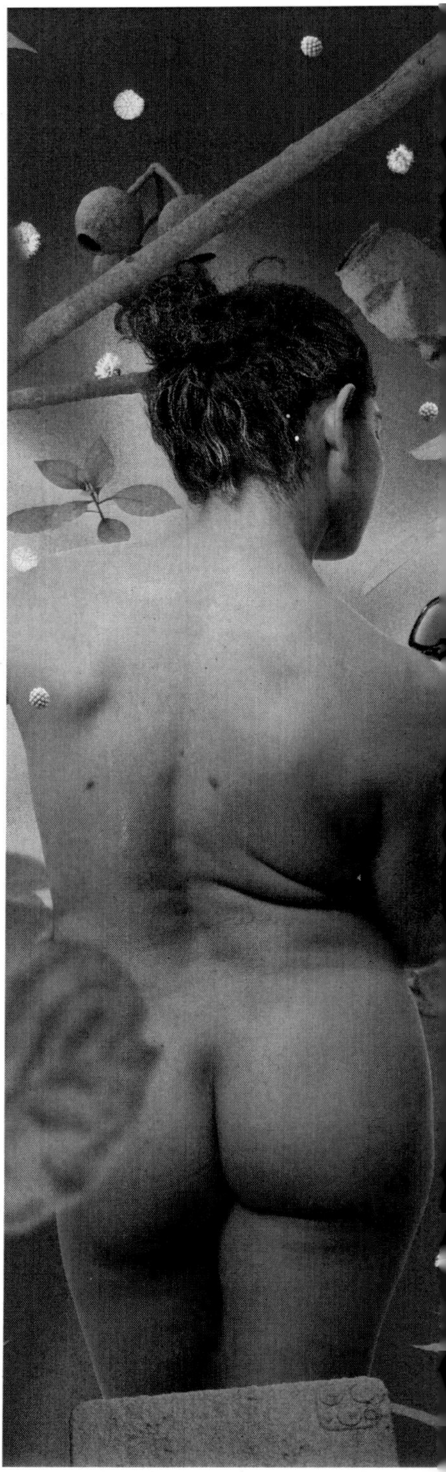

PRESENTING PARTNER

SYDNEY THEATRE COMPANY

SUPPORTED BY

GOVERNMENT PARTNERS

Naturism *was commissioned through the Incubator – NSW Theatre (Emerging) Fellowship in collaboration with Griffin Theatre Company in 2020. It was subsequently developed with the support of the Griffin Studio Workshop donors. The development was supported by Belvoir St Theatre and was supported through a residency at Theatre and Performance Studies, the University of Sydney. The premiere production of* Naturism *is supported by Griffin's Production Partner program.*

PLAYWRIGHT'S NOTE

Now, I know what you're thinking. Which particular combination of synapses fired in this woman's brain that caused her to write such a bizarre and naked piece of theatre? Well, dear reader, just because you asked, I'll dish the dirty details.

The year was 2019. The setting was the beautiful Sunshine Coast, where my partner **Kurt** and I were staying with his family. As our plane made its descent, I spied plumes of smoke peppering the hills of the temperate rainforest, and I remember anticipating that perhaps our relaxing escape might not be as carefree as we hoped.

Kurt's aunt and uncle's property backs onto a beautiful creek rich with Australian fauna and flora. Koalas regularly curl up in the gum trees in their backyard. For the first few days of our stay we caught mud crabs among the mangroves and lazed on the peaceful, but albeit dry and hazy, beaches around Noosa. But one afternoon, I was awoken from a nap at the house by an automated text from the RFS and a disorienting orange glow cast on the bedroom walls. I groggily emerged and found **Uncle Ben** packing go bags and hosing the roof of the house. We watched and waited as helicopters sloshed water from the nearby creek hopelessly against the approaching front of bushfire. We got the text as fat, dove grey ashes began to fall like snowflakes onto our clothes. EVACUATE NOW.

We were evacuated for three days as we nervously awaited news of the house. We tried to swim and drink beers to self-soothe, but everything felt... hollow. When we were allowed to return, thankfully, the house was saved, but the fire had totally destroyed the bushland between the property line and the creek. What was, just three days prior, thriving wetlands too marshy to walk on in places was now blackened, cracked earth, dotted with nothing but burnt out logs—some still housing pathetic little spot fires.

Kurt and I took Uncle Ben's canoe and a laundry bucket and paddled down the creek to look at the devastation. When we saw a spot fire, we'd park up at the bank and douse it out as best we could. We paddled past a journalist and photographer who said they were from the Courier Mail, and we were interviewed for a story! You can google it if you like... but be warned that instead of looking like Audrey Tautou in Amélie, I looked more like Lord Farquaad from Shrek (turns out that straightening one's hair is really low on the list of evacuation priorities). To make matters worse, the journo misspelled my name, so as far as Queensland print media is concerned, I am "Arg Collins", the heroic bucket-bearing playwright.

But my newsworthy misfortune had a silver lining. It made all of us—me, Kurt, Uncle Ben and **Aunty Lisa**—all completely lose our shit laughing. We were crying, wheezing and riffing with hilarious caveman bits ("Arg save house from fires!") for the whole final night of our stay. Even though we were eating dinner overlooking the undeniable devastation of this fiery close call, this fucking funny thing had come out of it. Multiple things can be true, I guess.

This, and the 2019/2020 summer of bushfires, replete with months of ashen ocean swims and smoke-soaked laundry drying on my balcony, was the kernel of inspiration behind *Naturism*. I read so many headlines speculating about the end of the world and Australia's future uninhabitability, about burnt koalas and coal in parliament and

PLAYWRIGHT'S NOTE

school children writing witty signs and skipping class. My brain (all our brains) were (and still are) being barraged with enough cognitively dissonant information to make anyone's neural pathways melt and stretch. *Naturism* in many ways is about this oxymoronic mode of contemporary existence.

And also, I just think we should remember we all have bodies buried under this mountain of stuff.

There's so much more I could say about writing this play, but instead I'll thank the many people who have helped shape its journey to the stage.

Firstly, *Naturism*'s development would not have been possible without the generous support of Create NSW and the Incubator Fellowship. In partnership with Create NSW, Griffin Theatre Company backed this wackadoo idea right from the start, and have consistently provided support (financial, dramaturgical, professional) to me and the play for more than five years. Thanks also to Belvoir St Theatre and the Inner West Council for additional development support.

Uncle Ben and Aunty Lisa's property has welcomed koalas back in the years since the fires, and they generously offered me the chance to use the house as a writing retreat in 2023, where I wrote important drafts of the work.

Tessa Leong was instrumental in the early development of this work as its first dramaturg. Thanks for the notes, the friendship and the swims!

Many wonderful actors have lent their talents to this play along the way. Thank you to **Danny Adcock, Camila Ponte Alvarez, Blazey Best, Nicholas Brown, Jeremi Campese, Peter Carroll, Nick Drummond, Glenn Hazeldine, Melissa Kahraman, Bec Massey, Arky Michael, Fraser Morrison, Johnny Nasser, Sam O'Sullivan, Anthony Taufa, Cat Văn-Davies, Nikita Waldron and Hannah Waterman**. You've all collectively given me abs because of how much you've made me laugh, so you can add that to your résumés, if you'd like.

I'd also like to thank my Mum and Dad for their parental dramaturgical insights, to **Georgie** and **Katie** for being up for visiting nude beaches with me during the play's research period, to **Lewis** for being my comedy hero, to **Lizzie**, **Kurt**, **Phillip**, **Eve**, **Georgie**, **Katie**, **Madee**, **Julia**, **Whitney**, **Thomas**, **Nathan**, **Peter** & **Dianne** and **Jake**. Thanks to my agent **Sharne McGee**, and to my former agent **Sally McLennan**.

Finally, a ridiculous amount of thanks must go to **Declan Greene** for the countless hours of dramaturgical support, directorial panache, (mostly) hilarious gag offers, and (always) invaluable lessons in story. Thank you thank you!

Sincerely,
~~Arg Collins~~ Ang Collins
Playwright

BIOGRAPHIES

ANG COLLINS

PLAYWRIGHT

Ang is a writer, dramaturg and game designer from Newcastle whose work has been seen on stages across Australia. Recent credits include: for Griffin Theatre Company (Batch Festival): *You've Got Mail*; for BBT/Red Line Productions at the Old Fitz: *Chorus*; for Civic Theatre Newcastle/Lingua Franca: *Blueberry Play*; for Meat Market Stables/ Periscope Productions: *Huge Indoor Plant Warehouse Sale*, *Old Friends*; for New Annual: *Spewy*; for New Annual/Whale Chorus Theatre Company: *Meet Me at the Baths*; for Wagga Wagga Art Gallery/Wagga Wagga Civic Theatre: *said han*.

Ang's debut play, *Blueberry Play*, was shortlisted for the 2017 Griffin Award, premiered at Griffin Theatre Company's Batch Festival in 2018 and has enjoyed several successful seasons across Australia.

Ang has received a variety of prestigious awards and opportunities, including a residency at the Inner West Council in 2022, the 2020/2021 Incubator Fellowship for Create NSW/Griffin Theatre Company and Create NSW's Young Creative Leaders Fellowship. Ang is a performing company member of acclaimed arts-science collective Boho Interactive. She holds a Bachelor of Arts (Languages) from the University of Sydney, and a Master of Fine Arts (Writing for Performance) from NIDA.

BIOGRAPHIES

DECLAN GREENE

DIRECTOR & DRAMATURG

Griffin Theatre Company: *Dogged*, *Green Park*, *Sex Magick* (co-directed with Nicholas Brown), *The Lewis Trilogy*, *Whitefella Yella Tree* (co-directed with Amy Sole); Sydney Theatre Company: *Hamlet, Prince of Skidmark*; Griffin Theatre Company and Hayes Theatre Co: *Flat Earthers: The Musical*; Malthouse Theatre: *Wake in Fright*; for Malthouse Theatre and Sydney Theatre Company: *Blackie Blackie Brown*; ZLMD Shakespeare Company: *Conviction*. As a playwright: *Eight Gigabytes of Hardcore Pornography*, *The Homosexuals, or 'Faggots'*, *Melancholia*, *Pompeii L.A. and Moth*.

Declan co-founded queer experimental theatre company Sisters Grimm with Ash Flanders in 2006, and has directed and co-created all their productions to date, including: for Griffin Independent and Theatre Works: *Summertime in the Garden of Eden*; for Malthouse Theatre and Sydney Theatre Company: *Calpurnia Descending*; for Melbourne Theatre Company: *Lilith: The Jungle Girl*; and for Sydney Theatre Company: *Little Mercy*. He was previously Resident Artist at Malthouse Theatre.

BIOGRAPHIES

CHLOË DALLIMORE

INTIMACY & MOVEMENT DIRECTOR

Chloë is an internationally trained and accredited Intimacy Coordinator/Director. Theatre: Griffin Theatre Company: *Blaque Showgirls, Sex Magick*; Griffin Theatre Company/Hayes Theatre Co: *Flat Earthers: The Musical*; Belvoir St Theatre: *At What Cost?, Big Girls Don't Cry, Miss Peony, The Master & Margarita* ; Crossroads Live: *Annie, CATS, Jesus Christ Superstar, The Rocky Horror Picture Show* ; Hayes Theatre Co: *Jekyll and Hyde, The Pirates of Penzance, Ride The Cyclone, Zombie! The Musical*; Opera Australia: *Amadeus, Miss Saigon, RENT*, Summer Season '25, Winter Season '25; Sydney Theatre Company: *A Fool In Love, Dear Evan Hansen, The Importance of Being Earnest, The Seagull, The Talented Mr Ripley*. Film: *I Know What You Did Last Summer (2025), Transfusion (2023)*. Television: Binge: *Mix Tape, Strife, The Last Anniversary, The Twelve* ; Netflix: *Heartbreak High, Wellmania*; Paramount+: *Last King of the Cross, NCIS: Sydney, Playing Gracie Darling*; Stan: *Bump, Colin From Accounts*. Chloë received the Australian Entertainment Mo Award for Female Musical Theatre Performer (2004), the Helpmann Award for Best Female Actor in a Musical (2005), the Sydney Theatre Award for Best Actress in a Supporting Role (2005), the Victorian Green Room Association Awards for Best Leading Female Artist in Music Theatre (2005).

JAMES BROWNE

DESIGNER

Griffin Theatre Company: *Beached*, *Diving for Pearls*, *Ladies Day*; Crossroads Live: *Cluedo, Grease*; CDP Theatre: *Tim*, *Turns*; Comedy Theatre: *Midnight*; David Venn Enterprises: *Cruel Intentions*; Ensemble Theatre: *Half Life of Marie Curie*, *Primary Trust*, *The Great Divide*; Hayes Theatre Co: *Cabaret*, *Xanadu*; Iconic Productions Children's Theatre: *Josephine Wants to Dance*, *Pete the Sheep*, *Spot*, *The Very Hungry Caterpillar*, *Yong*; Merrigong Theatre Company: *Letters to Lindy*; National Theatre of Parramatta (NT ofP): *Guards at the Taj*, *Karim*; Sydney Opera House: *Blanc de Blanc*, *Cirque Stratosphere*, *Hair, Velvet*; Theatre Creation Japan: *Ghost*; Victorian Opera: *The Selfish Giant*. Awards: Best Costume Design 2020 Broadway World Sydney Awards *(Hair)*. Nominations in the Australian Production Design Awards, Green Room Awards and Sydney Theatre Awards. Training: Theatre Design at the Western Australian Academy of Performing Arts (WAAPA) and Australian Film Television and Radio School (AFTRS) in Art Direction.

BIOGRAPHIES

VERITY HAMPSON

LIGHTING DESIGNER

Verity's lighting designs for theatre include: for Griffin Theatre Company: *Nucleus*, *Blaque Showgirls*, *A Strategic Plan*, *And No More Shall We Part*, *Angela's Kitchen*, *Beached*, *Dealing With Clair*, *Dogged*, *Ghosting the Party*, *Orange Thrower*, *Pony*, *The Bleeding Tree*, *The Boys*, *The Bull, The Moon and the Coronet of Stars*; for Griffin Independent: *The Brothers Size*, *The Cold Child*, *Crestfall*, *Family Stories: Belgrade*, *Live Acts On Stage*, *Music*, *The New Electric Ballroom*; for Griffin/Bell Shakespeare: *The Literati*; for Sydney Theatre Company: *7 Stages of Grieving*, *A Raisin in the Sun*, *Blackie Blackie Brown*, *Fences*, *Grand Horizons*, *Hamlet: Prince of Skidmark*, *Home*, *I'm Darling*, *Machinal*, *Little Mercy*; for Bell Shakespeare: *Henry V*, *Twelfth Night*, *A Midsummer Night's Dream*, *Julius Caesar*, *Titus Andronicus*; for Belvoir St Theatre: *An Enemy of the People*, *The Blind Giant is Dancing*, *The Drover's Wife*; for Black Swan/Sydney Theatre Company: *City of Gold*; for Ensemble Theatre: *A Doll's House*, *Baby Doll*, *Fully Committed*, *Murder at Hamlington Hall*, *Primary Trust*, *The Glass Menagerie*, *The Half-Life of Marie Curie*, *The Heartbreak Choir*, *The One*; for Hayes Theatre Co: *Lizzie*, *Zombie! The Musical*; for Melbourne Theatre Company: *The Black Woman of Gippsland*; for Queensland Theatre: *Death of a Salesman*.

Verity is a recipient of the Mike Walsh Fellowship and has won three Sydney Theatre Awards, a Green Room Award and an APDG Award for Best Lighting Design.

BIOGRAPHIES

DAVID BERGMAN

COMPOSER & SOUND DESIGNER

David's designs for theatre include: for Griffin Theatre Company: sound designer *Green Park*, composer and sound designer *Superheroes*, composer, sound, and video designer *First Love Is The Revolution*; for Bell Shakespeare: sound designer *Twelfth Night*, *The Lovers*: for Belvoir St Theatre: composer and sound designer *Scenes From The Climate Era*, sound designer *Into The Woods*, video designer *Blue*, sound designer *At What Cost?*; for Ensemble Theatre: composer and sound designer *Aria, Memory Of Water*; for Hayes Theatre Co: sound and video designer *Merrily We Roll Along*, sound designer *Dubbo Championship Wrestling*, *The Rise And Disguise Of Elizabeth R.*, *Catch Me If You Can*, *Spring Awakening*; for Michael Cassel Group: video design *Dear Evan Hansen*; for Monkey Baa Theatre; video designer *Possum Magic*, *The Peasant Prince*, sound designer *Josephine Wants To Dance*; for Soft Tread: video and sound design *The Gospel According To Paul*; for Sydney Theatre Company: video designer *The Picture of Dorian Gray*, *Strange Case of Dr Jekyll and Mr Hyde*, sound design *Playing Beatie Bow*, video and sound design *A Cheery Soul and The Wharf Revue* (from 2009-2018), video design *Julius Caesar*, *Muriel's Wedding: The Musical*, *The Hanging, The Effect*, *The Long Way Home*. David has won two Sydney Theatre Company awards: for Best Stage Design of a Mainstage Production for *The Picture of Dorian Gray* and for Best Sound Design of a Mainstage Production for *Green Park*.

BIOGRAPHIES

LILY HAYMAN

ASSOCIATE DIRECTOR

Lily is a writer, director and producer from Southern Sydney who lives and works on the unceded land of the Dharawal people and is passionate about new Australian work. Lily's directing credits include; for Purple Tape Productions: *[YOUR NAME]*, *Party Girl*, *Expiration Date*, *Fledgling and The Infinity Mirror*; for Shopfront Arts Co-Op *The Future Show*, *Dignified Exit and Stop. Drop. And Listen*. As Assistant Director; for Milk Crate Theatre: *DUST*. As Producer; For Brisbane Festival, Associate Producer: Activations and Installations 2025, for Purple Tape Productions; *werkaholics*, *[YOUR NAME]*, *Party Girl*, *Maa Ki Rasoi*, *Come Again*, *Tape Over Festival*, *Expiration Date*, *Fledgling and The Infinity Mirror*; for Operated Coin; *Garden of Sound*, *Chatterbot Chatterbot*; for Shopfront Arts Co-Op; Associate Producer 2021 - 25. She is the co-founder of Purple Tape Productions and the recipient of the KXT David Barthur Fellowship.

This role is proudly funded by NSW Government.

CHLOE LANGDON

STAGE MANAGER

Chloe Langdon is a Sydney-based Stage Manager and AV Technician.

For Griffin Theatre Company, as Stage Manager: *Naturism*. As Production & Technical Coordinator: *Nucleus*.

For Sydney Theatre Company, as Assistant Stage Manager: *Dracula*, *Happy Days*, *On The Beach*, *The Seagull*. As Mic Technician: *Dear Evan Hansen*, *Do Not Go Gentle*, *The Dictionary of Lost Words*, *The Importance of Being Earnest*, *The Lifespan of a Fact*, *The Strange Case of Dr. Jekyll & Mr Hyde*, *The Talented Mr. Ripley*. As Sound Support: *RBG: Of Many, One, The President*. As Stage Management Support: *A Fool in Love*, *Julia*, *The President*.

Other credits include: for Sydney Chamber Opera, as AV Systems Technician: *Aphrodite*; for Sydney Festival, as Mic Technician: *William Yang: Milestone*, *The Chronicles*; for Crossroads Live, as Mic Technician: *ELF! The Musical*.

BIOGRAPHIES

NICHOLAS BROWN

SID

NIDA graduate Nicholas Brown has forged an impressive international career across film, television and theatre as an actor, writer, singer, songwriter and leading man with major roles in Bollywood films, Australian drama and as a much-loved ABC Play School presenter. His theatre acting credits include for Belvoir St Theatre: *Counting And Cracking, The Curious Incident Of The Dog In The Night-Time*; for New Theatricals: *Come From Away*; for Queensland Theatre: *Bernhardt/Hamlet, Taming of the Shrew*; for Sydney Theatre Company: *Circle Mirror Transformation, Still Point Turning, The Long Forgotten Dream*. Film and TV credits include Alex Proyas's *R.U.R*, Paramount+: *Fake*, Picture Works Australia:*Sahela*, ABC: *In Our Blood*, Lingo Pictures: *Upright* (Season 2), Fremantle: *The PM's Daughter* and Nine Network: *Amazing Grace*. Nicholas won the Nick Enright Prize for Playwriting in the 2024 NSW Premier's Literary Awards for his play *Sex Magick* which was performed in the 2023 Griffin Theatre Company season. It was also nominated for a 2025 AWGIE and a 2024 Sydney Theatre Award. His other self-penned play *Lighten Up* was part of the Griffin season in 2016. Nicholas's life story has been recently featured on ABC Conversations: A wild Bollywood adventure—from Sydney to Mumbai and back again.

BIOGRAPHIES

GLENN HAZELDINE

RAY

Griffin Theatre Company: *Porn.Cake.*; Griffin Theatre Company/ La Boite Theatre: *A Hoax*; Darlinghurst Theatre Company: *Every Second, Lawrence and Holloman*; Ensemble Theatre: *Rhinestone Rex and Miss Monica, David Williamson's Jack Manning Trilogy, Managing Carmen, Rapture Blister Burn, The Ruby Sunrise, Tuesdays with Morrie, A View from the Bridge, Birthrights, All My Sons*; Melbourne Theatre Company/Sydney Theatre Company: *Così, The Father, Don's Party*; Merrigong Theatre Company: *As Luck Would Have It, Letters to Lindy*; Queensland Theatre: *Rhinestone Rex & Miss Monica*; Sydney Theatre Company: *No Pay? No Way!, Blithe Spirit, Away, Disgraced, Arcadia, After Dinner, Perplexed, Love and Information, Tot Mom, Elling, The Pig Iron People, Julius Caesar, Victory, Dead White Males; Bell Shakespeare: As You Like It*; Company B Belvoir: *The Judas Kiss*; Red Line Productions: *Amadeus, Death of a Salesman*; Seymour Centre: *Museum of Modern Love, Transparency*.

Film: *Fangs, Dripping in Chocolate, Last Cab to Darwin, Last Train to Freo, Little Monsters*; Television: *A Place to Call Home, All Saints, ANZAC Girls, Colin from Accounts 1&2, House of Bond, Redfern Now, The Elegant Gentleman's Guide to Knife Fighting, The Moodys, The Twelve, Water Rats*.

Training: *NIDA Graduate*; Positions: *NSW President of Actors Equity, Deputy Chair of Actors Benevolent Fund NSW.*

BIOGRAPHIES

FRASER MORRISON

ADAM

Fraser Morrison is a Sydney-based actor who studied at École Philippe Gaulier. Theatre credits include Belvoir St Theatre: *Grief is The Thing With Feathers*; Fruit Box Theatre: *Cruise*; Old Fitz Theatre: *The Eisteddfod*; Legit Theatre: *Dumb Kids*; KXT/CrissCross Productions: *Cherry Smoke, Natives*; ATYP: *The Resistance, M.Rock*; Outhouse Theatre Company: *How to Defend Yourself*; Darlinghurst Theatre Company: *Remembering Pirates*; Metro Arts: *Reagan Kelly*. His screen highlights include Disney+: *The Last Days of the Space Age*; SBS: *The Family Law*; CIMP Productions: *Oi* which premiered at MIFF.

CAMILA PONTE ALVAREZ

EVANGELINE

Camila's recent theatre credits include: for La Boite Theatre/Riverside Theatres: *Yoga Play*; for National Theatre of Parramatta: *Fade*. Her screen credits include: for Paramount+: *Last King of the Cross*; for ABC: *Barons*; for Nine Network: *Amazing Grace*, *Doctor Doctor*; for Seven Network: *Home & Away*, *RFDS: Royal Flying Doctor Service*; for Amenta Network: *Ms Vanguard*.

Born in Tablelands Queensland to Venezuelan Parents, Camila started as a dancer, until she completed her schooling at Newtown High School of the Performing Arts and was later accepted to Western Australian Academy of Performing Arts where she completed her Acting degree in 2019.

BIOGRAPHIES

HANNAH WATERMAN

HELEN

Training: National Youth Theatre of Great Britain. University of Warwick, Bachelor of Arts (English & Theatre) 1996. Theatre: Griffin Theatre Company: *The Almighty Sometimes*, *Wicked Sisters*; Belvoir St Theatre: *The Spare Room*; CDP: *Mr Stink*: Ensemble Theatre: *The Kitchen Sink*, *Summer of Harold*, *Colder than Here*; Hit Productions: *Love Letters*; Michael Cassell Group: *Mary Poppins*, *Harry Potter and The Cursed Child*; One Eyed Man Productions: *Side Show*; Red Line Productions: *The Whale*; Sydney Theatre Company: *Talk*. Film: *Mercy Road*, *Patient 17*, *The Nightingale*. Television (Australia): Channel 9: *Bali 2002*, *Home and Away*; Endemol Shine Australia: NCIS SYDNEY; (UK) *Eastenders*, *New Tricks*, *Tess of The D'urbervilles*, *The Afternoon Play*, *The Bill*, *Trial and Retribution*. Awards & Nominations: Winner of the National Shakespeare on a Platform Competition (New Globe Theatre) 1993, nominated for Best Supporting Actress in *The Almighty Sometimes* (GLUGS) 2018.

A proud member of Actors Equity.

ABOUT GRIFFIN

Griffin is the only theatre company in the country exclusively devoted to the development and staging of new Australian writing. Located in the historic SBW Stables Theatre, nestled in the heart of Kings Cross, Griffin has been Australia's home for the exploration of new stories since 1979.

We are the launch pad for new plays, ideas and writing that other theatres won't take a risk on. We boldly contribute to Australia's unique and powerful storytelling culture. Plays like *Prima Facie, Holding the Man* and *City of Gold* all had their world premieres at Griffin before going out to capture the national imagination. In the words of our longest-serving Artistic Director, **Ros Horin**:

"We are the theatre of first chances."

We are passionate about nurturing emerging and established practitioners alike. We pride ourselves on supporting our vast community of artists, audiences and supporters who consider our theatre their creative home. We help ambitious, bold, risk-taking and urgent Australian work get from the page onto the stage. We tell the stories that help us know who we are as a nation and who we want to become.

Acknowledgement of Country

Griffin Theatre Company operates and tells stories on the unceded lands of the Gadigal of the Eora Nation. We acknowledge and honour Aboriginal and Torres Strait Islander people as the oldest continuous living culture on the planet, with more than 60,000 years of storytelling practice shaping and underpinning all aspects of Australian culture. It is a privilege that we do not take lightly: to work on this land, and to tell stories on its soil.

GRIFFIN THEATRE COMPANY
13 Craigend St
Gadigal Land, Kings Cross, NSW 2011

CONTACTS
02 9332 1052
info@griffintheatre.com.au
griffintheatre.com.au

GRIFFIN FAMILY

Board
Bruce Meagher (Chair)
Guillaume Babille
Nigel Barrington
Simon Burke AO
Julieanne Campbell
Jane Clifford
Declan Greene
Julia Pincus
Lenore Robertson AM
Simone Whetton

Artistic Director and Co-CEO
Declan Greene

Executive Director and Co-CEO
Julieanne Campbell

General Manager
Khym Scott

Literary Associate
Daley Rangi

Senior Producer
Emily David

Associate Producers
Cassie Hamilton
Whitney Richards

Head of Development
Jake Shavikin

Relationship Manager
Harry Lyddiard

Marketing Manager
Erica Penollar

Marketing and Content Producer
Christie Yip

Ticketing Manager
Gavin Roach

Ticketing Administrator
Nathan Harrison

Front of House Manager
Alex Bryant-Smith

Front of House
Riordan Berry,
Max Philips,
Maddy Withington

Administrator
Blake Hahn

Production Manager
Jimi Rawlings

Production and Technical Coordinator
Amy Norton

Finance Manager
Chrissy Riley

Finance Consultant
Emma Murphy

Project Officer
Heather Tleige

Publicity
Kabuku PR

Graphic Design
Susu Studio

Cover Photography
Brett Boardman

Web Developer
DevQuoll

SYDNEY THEATRE COMPANY

One of the world's largest not-for-profit theatre producers, Sydney Theatre Company is at the heart of Australia's cultural landscape. It owes its world class creative pedigree to a history of ground-breaking productions.

Since 1978, the Company has produced work that is – in the words of founding Artistic Director Richard Wherrett – "grand, vulgar, intelligent, challenging, and fun". A paradox as playful as our city.

We are proud that over the years Sydney Theatre Company has produced work with some of Australia's – and the world's – most exciting performers, writers, directors and creative teams; and that we continue to invest in the artistic legends of the future.

Learn more and book tickets at **sydneytheatre.com.au**

Artistic Director & Co-CEO
Mitchell Butel

Executive Director & Co-CEO
Anne Dunn

Head of Public Relations & Communications
Helene Fox

Chief External Relations Officer
Danielle Heidbrink

Director, Technical & Production
Andrew Mackonis

Director People & Safety
Bettina Sammut

Director, Finance & Governance
Penny Scaiff

Chief Operating Officer
Caroline Spence

Senior Producer
Ben White

Director, Digital Innovation
Heath Wilder

Director, Marketing
Sophie Withers

sydneytheatre.com.au
Wharf 4/5, 15 Hickson Rd,
Walsh Bay NSW 2000
(02) 9250 1777
mail@sydneytheatre.com.au
@sydneytheatreco

Sign up to our monthly enews at sydneytheatre.com.au/enews

Sydney Theatre Company acknowledges the Gadigal of the Eora nation who are the traditional custodians of the land and waters on which the Company gathers. We pay our respects to Elders past and present, and we extend that respect to all Aboriginal and Torres Strait Islander people with whom we work and with whom we share stories.

GRIFFIN DONORS

Income from Griffin activities covers less than 40% of our operating costs—leaving an ever-increasing gap for us to fill through government funding, sponsorship and the generosity of our individual supporters. Your support helps us bridge the gap and keep ticket prices affordable and our work at its best.

To make a donation and a difference, contact Griffin on **(02) 9332 1052** *or donate online at* **griffintheatre.com.au/support**

PROGRAM PATRONS

Griffin Ambassadors
Robertson Foundation

Griffin Amplify
Girgensohn Foundation

Griffin Literary Associate
Malcolm Robertson Foundation
Robertson Foundation

Griffin Redraft Fund
Shane & Cathryn Brennan

Suzie Miller Award
Suzie Miller

Griffin Studio
Gil Appleton
Darin Cooper Foundation
Corinne & Bryan
Kiong Lee & Richard Funston
Malcolm Robertson Foundation
Pip Rath & Wayne Lonergan
Geoff & Wendy Simpson AM
Danielle Smith & Sean Carmody

Griffin Studio Workshop
Shane & Cathryn Brennan (Patron)
Mary Ann Rolfe (Founding Patron)
Iolanda Capodanno & Juergen Krufczyk
Darin Cooper Foundation
Bob & Chris Ernst
Jane-Maree Hurley
Susan MacKinnon
Jake Shavikin
Merilyn Sleigh & Raoul de Ferranti

Griffin Women's Initiative
Nicole Abadee
Katrina Barter
Julieanne Campbell
Iolanda Capodanno
Jane Clifford
Jennifer Darin
Eveline Dowling
Mandy Foley
Nicola Forrest AO
Melinda Graham
Sherry Gregory
Rosemary Hannah & Lynette Preston
Page Henty
Jane-Maree Hurley
Tessa Leong
Susan MacKinnon
Sophie McCarthy
Suzie Miller
Naomi Parry
Julia Pincus
Jo Porter
Ruth Ritchie
Lenore Robertson AM
Ann Sloan
Deanne Weir
Simone Whetton
Ali Yeldham
Anonymous (1)

PRODUCTION PARTNERS 2025

Naturism by Ang Collins
Darin Cooper Foundation
Robert Dick & Erin Shiel
Mandy Foley
Rosemary Hannah & Lynette Preston
Kate Morgan
Bruce Meagher & Greg Waters
Julia Pincus & Ian Learmonth

PRODUCTION PARTNERS 2024

The Lewis Trilogy by Louis Nowra
Darin Cooper Foundation
Robert Dick & Erin Shiel
Rosemary Hannah & Lynette Preston
Kate Morgan
Bruce Meagher & Greg Waters
Julia Pincus & Ian Learmonth
Seaborn, Broughton & Walford Foundation

SEASON DONORS

Company Patrons $100,000+
Shane & Cathryn Brennan
Neilson Foundation

Season Patrons $50,000-$99,999
Malcolm Robertson Foundation
Robertson Foundation

Mainstage Donors $20,000-$49,999
Darin Cooper Foundation
Girgensohn Foundation
Robert Dick & Erin Shiel
Rosemary Hannah & Lynette Preston
Julia Pincus & Ian Learmonth
Sally Breen Family Foundation
Anonymous (1)

Production Donors $10,000-$19,999
Jenny Ainsworth
Carla Zampatti Foundation
Doc Ross Family Foundation
Gordon & Marie Esden
Ingrid Kaiser
Kate Morgan
Bruce Meagher & Greg Waters
Suzie Miller
Kate Morgan
Mountain Air Foundation
The Myer Foundation
Rebel Penfold-Russell OAM
Geoff & Wendy Simpson AM
The Skrzynski Foundation
The Wales Family Foundation
The WeirAnderson Foundation

Rehearsal Donors $5,000–$9,999
Brian Abel & Mark Manton
Antoinette Albert
Gil Appleton
Lisa Barker & Don Russell
Margaret & Bernard Coles
Corinne & Bryan
Bob & Chris Ernst
Stephen Fitzgerald
Carrillo Gantner AC & Ziyin Gantner
Danny Gilbert AM & Kathleen Gilbert
Elizabeth Hurst
Lambert Bridge Foundation
Kiong Lee & Richard Funston
Polese Foundation
Pip Rath & Wayne Lonergan
Merilyn Sleigh & Raoul de Ferranti
Danielle Smith & Sean Carmody

DONORS CONTINUED

Final Draft Donors $3,000–$4,999
Melissa Ball
Baly Douglass Foundation
Iolanda Capodanno
& Juergen Krufczyk
Sherry Gregory
John Head
Jane-Maree Hurley
Susan MacKinnon
Anthony Paull

Workshop Donors $1,000–$2,999
Nicole Abadee & Rob Macfarlan
Emily Aitken
Katrina Barter
Cherry & Peter Best
Helen Bowden
Stephen & Annabelle Burley
Julieanne Campbell
Anna Cleary
Jane Clifford
Max Dingle OAM
Eveline Dowling
Ari Droga
Toby Duffy
Brian Everingham
John & Libby Fairfax
Nicholas & Rowena Falzon
Sandra & Rupert Ferman
Mandy Foley
Sandra Forbes
Melinda Graham
Peter Graves Canberra
Reg Graycar
Mink Greene
Lisa Hamilton & Rob White
Kate Harrison
Page Henty
Libby Higgin & Gae Anderson
Mark Hopkinson & Michelle Opie
David Hoskins & Paul McKnight
Susan Hyde
Colleen Kane
Adrienne & David Kitching
Tessa Leong
John Lewis
Helen Lochhead AO
Patricia Lynch
Matthew & Josephine
Sophie McCarthy
Sandra & Kent McPhee
Naomi Parry
Ian Phipps
Jo Porter
Andrew Post & Susan Quill
Kate Richardson & Chris Marrable
Steve Riethoff
In memory of Katherine Robertson
Sylvia Rosenblum
Jake Shavikin
Jann Skinner
Ann & Quinn Sloan
Geoffrey Starr
Arahni Sont
Leslie Stern
Martyn Thompson
Sue Thomson
Samantha Turley & Diego Silva
Janet Wahlquist
Richard Weinstein & Richard Benedict
Simone Whetton
David Williamson AO & Kristin Williamson
Ali Yeldham
Anonymous (7)

Reading Donors $500–$999
Sally Beath
Alex Bowen & Catherine Sullivan
Alex Bryant-Smith
Jane Christensen
Nick & Carol Dettmann
Elizabeth Evatt
Erica Gray
Susi Hamilton
James Hartwright & Kerrin D'Arcy
Michael Jackson
Noella Lopez
Robert Marks
Simon Marrable
Christopher Matthies
& Graham Parsons
Siobahn Mullany
Jenni Neary AM
Virginia Pursell
A.O. Redmond
Steph Sands
Patricia Spinks
Adam Suckling
Fiona Thomas
Stuart Thomas
Michael Thompson OAM & Ian Kelly
Duncan Thomson
Julie Whitfield
Anonymous (4)

First Draft Donors $200-$499
Robyn Ayres
Edwina Birch
Caitlin Brass
David Caulfield
Sue Clark
Edward Cooper & Daniel Zucker
Joanne Court
Brendan Crotty
Bryan Cutler
Melita Daru
Rosemary Dermody
Peter & Lou Duerden
Paul & Jean Eagar
Kevin Farmer
Yvonne Fetherston
R Furley
Deane Golding
Peter Gray & Helen Thwaites
Wendy Gray
Sue Halloran & Jim Allen
Matthew Huxtable
Marian & Nabeel Ibrahim
David Lacey
Bronwyn Leece
Liz Locke
George & Maruschka Loupis
Duncan McKay
Dr Stephen McNamara
Margaret Murphy
Dian Neligan
Carolyn Newman
Sally Patten
Peter Pezzutti
Meredith Phelps
Belinda Piggott & David Ojerholm
Nick Read
Ann Rocca
Michael & Noelleen Rosen
David Russell
Kevin & Shirley Ryan
Jane S
Margaret Teh
Rosemary White
Yoda & Modgie
William Zappa
Ray Ziesing
Anonymous (13)

Griffin Friends Forever
We remember and honour those who have generously supported the future of Australian storytelling through a bequest to Griffin Theatre Company.

Thank you:
Annette Mary Lunney
Estate of the Late John William Roe

CURRENT AS OF 14 OCT 2025

GRIFFIN SPONSORS

Griffin would like to thank the following:

OUR PARTNERS

GOVERNMENT SUPPORTERS

PATRON

LEGACY BENEFACTOR

VENUE PARTNER

CREATIVE PARTNERS

SUSU STUDIO

GIRGENSOHN
FOUNDATION

COMPANY PARTNERS

All Things
All Creatures

bourke street bakery

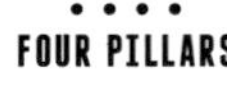

Griffin Theatre Company is assisted by the Australian Government through Creative Australia, its principal arts investment and advisory body.
Griffin Theatre Company is supported by the NSW Government through Create NSW.